Presented to

_____

On the Occasion of

_____

From

_____

Date

_____

DAILY
WISDOM
for
Couples

DEVOTIONAL JOURNAL FOR EVERY DAY

TONI SORTOR &
PAMELA MCQUADE

BARBOUR
PUBLISHING, INC.

Published by Barbour Publishing, Inc, P. O. Box 719, Uhrichsville, Ohio 44683
http://www.barbourbooks.com

 Member of the
Evangelical Christian
Publishers Association

Printed in Belgium.

DAILY WISDOM
WISDOM
for
Couples

Introduction

God created the institution of marriage. He offers marriage as a blessing to us, but our actual relationships are only what we make of them. When, through conscious effort, we put good things into them, our relationships will improve.

Daily Wisdom for Couples is designed to encourage married couples to insert positive elements into their relationships through Bible reading, prayer, and journaling. Through this book, readers will be challenged to consider how God's Word relates to their lives, and to practice His commands through weekend activities—each designed to improve communication and draw couples together.

We suggest that you begin using this devotional journal on the Monday of the appropriately numbered week after you receive the book. If, for example, you receive this journal as a Christmas gift, begin the devotionals on the first Monday of the new year (week 1). If you received the book as a wedding gift in early June, begin the devotionals on the Monday of week 23. This method will keep your devotional readings in the proper season of the year, tying in with holidays and special events as they occur.

The devotionals are grouped by weeks: The Monday through Saturday devotionals will prepare you for the Sunday activity, to be shared by each husband and wife. Most will take only a modest amount of time but will challenge readers to live out their faith. As you think over the daily devotionals and perform the weekly activities, write down what you've learned and how you've grown. Journaling space is provided with each day's selection, and additional writing space is included in the back of the book.

May this book bless you both as you read, write, and act.

When God told Isaac to take his wife and make his home in Egypt, Isaac obeyed, even though he was afraid for his life. In return for his faithfulness, the Lord blessed Isaac, increasing his investment a hundred times over in one year.

> Then Isaac sowed in that land, and received in the same year an hundredfold: and the Lord blessed him.
> GENESIS 26:12 KJV

What is God telling you and your spouse this year? Would you rather live somewhere else, do something else, even be someone else? Do you want to argue the point or pretend you didn't get the message, or are you willing to trust God's guidance and faithfulness? On this first day of a new year, take time as a couple to discuss where you think God wants you to be this year and what you hope He will help you accomplish in the next 365 days.

Father, we ask Your guidance for this new year,
confident that wherever You send us,
we will be protected and blessed.

> Then the Lord God said,
> "It is not good that
> the man should be alone;
> I will make him
> a helper as his partner."
> GENESIS 2:18 NRSV

Whatever this year may bring, you do not have to face it alone. You have a partner and a helper to rejoice with and receive strength from in good times and bad. This gives you an enormous advantage: What one of you cannot do, the other can; what one of you fears, the other does not.

To make the most of this advantage, you need to remember that you are partners in life. This means that sometimes you will lead and sometimes you will help. Both roles are equally important, and each member of the team will play both roles during the year.

Listen to your partner, discuss every decision together, and give thanks for the varying abilities you bring to your marriage. You will prosper as a team.

Lord, we realize that we are stronger and smarter when we work together on a problem. Please remind us of this any time we are tempted to "take over" or impose our own ways on each other. Help us use our own particular talents to grow as a team.

Since none of us is going to reach perfection during this lifetime, on occasion we will experience some fear in our relationships. For most, these fears will be minor: spending a little too much for an unnecessary luxury, gaining a little too much weight, making a decision without consulting the other, and so on. Actually, we don't fear our spouses' reactions as much as we wonder what they will think of us. Will they trust us as much as before?

> There is no fear in love, but perfect love casts out fear.
> 1 JOHN 4:18 NRSV

Learning to work as a team and trusting the other member takes time. As the years go by, we become more attuned to our partners. We discover what bugs them and what doesn't, and out of love—not fear—we adjust our actions. In time, there will be no fear between us, only patience and understanding.

Father, help us in this job of removing fear and uncertainty from our relationship. Help us to grow in confidence and love as a couple.

> Did the contempt of families terrify me, that I kept silence, and went not out of the door?
>
> JOB 31:34 KJV

Let's face it, not everyone in your family is going to love your spouse immediately. Most of them will accept your choice, but one or two may not be much more than civil, considering her or him "beneath you" for one reason or another.

Avoiding those critical family members because of fear or anger serves nothing. It is better to show up at family events and keep on smiling, even if you're seething inside. With time, your spouse will prove to be "good enough" through the strength of your marriage, shared family experiences, and any children you may be blessed with. We cannot demand acceptance from anyone; we have to earn it, one day at a time.

Father, give us the patience we need to become valued members of our spouse's family. With time, they will realize how good we are for each other.

_____
_____
_____
_____
_____
_____
_____
_____
_____
_____
_____

Marriage is hard work, especially when it's new. Who would have thought that squeezing the toothpaste in the middle could be the basis of a two-day fight? Or that such a buttoned-down husband would be incapable of putting his dirty shorts in the hamper? How could such a lovely woman go to bed in flannel, even in summer? The list goes on.

> "And you have persevered and have patience, and have labored for My name's sake and have not become weary."
> REVELATION 2:3 NKJV

If you can get over these little problems, you will have the foundation of a strong marriage. Still, patience and perseverance are required: You need to come to acceptable compromises without becoming weary and, at the same time, keep working on the little issues that drive you crazy.

Lord, we are determined that our marriage is not going to suffer because of petty annoyances. Remind us of this promise when we disagree, and show us how we can overcome our differences.

> "Can two walk together,
> unless they are agreed?"
> AMOS 3:3 NKJV

How long has it been since the two of you took an old-fashioned walk? Not a power walk, a jog, and certainly not a run, but a leisurely, rambling walk, just for the fun of it.

Granted, the weather may not be perfect for walking, but that only means your walk will be more private. If there's a thunderstorm or blizzard raging, head for the nearest mall, with no shopping allowed.

Remember, not every activity requires a goal, and not all of our leisure time should be productive. What about just getting out of the house to admire God's world and spend some time with the one you love? Hold hands, bump shoulders, giggle a lot, and talk about your hopes and dreams. Just the two of you.

*Father, help us realize that being together without purpose
can be a wonderful experience that draws us closer.*

This weekend, instead of spending your precious free time doing chores you couldn't get done during the week, why not reestablish some family bonds? Are you connected to the Internet? If so, it takes only minutes to compose a message and send it off to every family member who has an e-mail address.

For some reason, people who would never write a letter or pick up the telephone will immediately return an e-mail message. You will be amazed at how many replies you will have waiting for you the next time you check the mail. If you don't have everyone's electronic address, begin to build your family address book this weekend and share it with other family members. The technology for keeping in touch is available. Use it to strengthen your extended family.

> But avoid foolish controversies
> and genealogies and arguments
> and quarrels about the law,
> because they are unprofitable and useless.
> TITUS 3:9 NIV

Before falling in love, couples seldom have the time to discuss their stands on all possible "issues." Life simply doesn't work that way. We generally check out the most important qualities for compatibility—religion, political beliefs, personality—and leave the rest for later. This is not necessarily bad because, if you dig deeply enough, you could spend your life looking for the "perfect" spouse.

You're not perfect, after all, and sometimes you and your spouse will disagree. The book of Titus tells us that some of these disagreements just aren't worth fighting over. When, after a few minutes of discussion, it becomes obvious that neither of you is going to change the other's mind, you both have to back off and agree to disagree.

Lord, we realize that any two people will sometimes disagree.
Please teach us to recognize the point at which further discussion becomes
"unprofitable and useless" and have the sense to back off.

_____

_____

_____

_____

_____

_____

_____

_____

_____

_____

_____

_____

_____

Exactly how much does your spouse need to know about your past? What should you confess to before and during marriage? Unfortunately, no one has compiled an up-to-date list. Certainly, you must admit to any sin that might put your partner in moral or physical danger, but how "big" must a wrongdoing be to qualify? Even if you decide on total confession of all your past sins, you still have to make judgment calls. What about that crush on your sixth-grade teacher? Or the quarters you lifted from your mother's purse? Or the other person you once thought of marrying?

> O God, you know my folly;
> the wrongs I have done
> are not hidden from you.
> PSALM 69:5 NRSV

God knows every wrong you have ever committed, confessed or hidden. If your conscience is burdened, ask Him for guidance on what you need to reveal. Trust Him to indicate what needs to be shared and what would be better off unsaid.

Father, we all have our little secrets.
Help us to identify those we need to share with each other
and those that would only hurt our partners.

> Behold, I send you forth as
> sheep in the midst of wolves:
> be ye therefore wise as serpents,
> and harmless as doves.
> MATTHEW 10:16 KJV

Not everyone you meet as a couple will have your best interests at heart. Some will pretend to be friends with ulterior motives in mind, some will be cheats and liars, and still others will try to corrupt your relationship. But notice that Jesus did not say to isolate yourselves from the world. You should get out there and live your lives, using wariness, good judgment, and intelligence in your dealings with the world's wolves.

At the same time, you are to remain as harmless as doves, never lowering yourselves to the level of the wolves, and never striking out in retaliation. As a Christian couple, you may become a target, but no one says you have to stand there and wait for the bullet.

Father, our lifestyle is not that of the world,
and we may find ourselves in conflict with others because of our faith.
When we do, give us the wisdom to avoid being hurt and the strength not to hurt in return.

_____

_____

_____

_____

_____

_____

_____

_____

_____

_____

_____

_____

The idea of patience is not a popular one today. We are expected to be aggressive, to go out and get what we want when we want it. Those who wait patiently for the Lord to supply their needs are generally subject to ridicule.

> Wait on the LORD:
> be of good courage,
> and he shall strengthen thine heart:
> wait, I say, on the LORD.
> PSALM 27:14 KJV

The same is true in marriage. When we demand something from our spouse that he or she cannot deliver immediately, our first reaction is to turn away, to not be patient. If the disappointments and the turning away become habitual, our marriage is in deep trouble. Notice that the verse above does not say we will always get what we want. Instead, it promises that our hearts will be strengthened. We will learn to be patient—we will learn how to love—even when we do not receive what we think we want.

Lord, give us patience in the face of unmet needs, strengthen our hearts, and help us to wait on You.

_____FRIDAY_____

> Jesus Christ is the same yesterday, today, and forever.
>
> HEBREWS 13:8 NKJV

Change ambushes us all. Just when we think we know someone as deeply as possible, we may wake up one morning and wonder who is on the other side of the bed. It certainly isn't the person we married! The problem is, we may not like a particular facet of his or her personality that didn't show itself until now.

People change as they go through life, sometimes for the better and sometimes not. A person—or a marriage—that does not grow or change is in trouble. Don't let change frighten you. As you age, change usually leads to a better life for you both. Only Jesus is the same "yesterday, today, and forever."

*Father, we can see each other changing as our relationship progresses
and are uncertain how the changes will work out.
Sometimes this frightens us.
Give us the courage we need to welcome change and adapt to it
so we will both be free to become the people You mean us to be.*

_____

_____

_____

_____

_____

_____

_____

_____

_____

_____

Lazily lying in bed on the weekend, have you ever been tormented by a constant drip from a leaky rain gutter? You drift off to sleep only to be jarred awake by the next drop. Will it *never* end? You take your pillow and stretch out on the couch, but you can still hear it. It's just farther away now.

> A continual dripping
> on a very rainy day
> and a contentious woman are alike.
> PROVERBS 27:15 NKJV

Sometimes people irritate you the same way. Your husband or wife has a bone to pick with you, usually over something inconsequential such as mowing the lawn or going food shopping. For some reason, your spouse feels immediate action is required and just won't let it go. Drip, drip, drip! The only way to escape the irritation is to mow the lawn and fix the drip. Yes, those we love can drive us buggy, and two people can disagree on what is important. When that happens to you, do you have the grace to give in with a smile and bring peace to the family?

Father, when we get on each other's nerves,
give us both the patience we need to deal with the problem and stop nagging each other.
If something is that vital to our spouse, we need to be able to give in with a smile.

It's time to make a list. On separate sheets of paper, write down the little things that bug you the most. This is not the time to start an argument; it's time to share some things you may not have put into words before. The rules are as follows:

1. Keep your list free of emotion. Don't say, "You never. . ." or "I hate. . . ."

2. Avoid hurting the other with such comments as "You sit like a lump all week-end," or "You've gained twenty pounds this year."

3. Make suggestions for the immediate future, such as "I would like to get out and do something together this weekend," or "I want to join a gym together. It'll be fun."

4. Go over your lists together. Explain anything that seems unclear to your spouse.

5. Decide what can be done and what cannot, and then decide where to start.

6. Toss the lists in the fireplace or wastebasket and go out for dinner.

The couple that shares a belief in Jesus also shares the peace of Jesus—and the mystery of that peace. On the surface such a couple may not seem to have anything but trouble, yet they are happy and content, willing to share the little they do have. As Jesus told His disciples, He does not give as the world gives, but He does give peace.

"Peace I leave with you;
my peace I give you.
I do not give to you as the world gives.
Do not let your hearts be troubled
and do not be afraid."
JOHN 14:27 NIV

Unbelievers who see such a couple are mystified. It makes no sense to them how, lacking in material possessions, two people can be at peace and living full, happy lives. For unbelievers the mystery will never be solved. But for Christians there is no secret to such a couple's happiness.

Father, sometimes the simplest gifts are too complex to comprehend.
Whenever possible, help us share the secret of our contentment with those who
do not understand Your peace and blessings.

> "And I will do whatever
> you ask in my name,
> so that the Son may bring glory to the Father.
> You may ask me for anything in my name,
> and I will do it."
> JOHN 14:13–14 NIV

Sometimes we forget what the real aim of our prayers should be. Jesus said we may ask for anything, spiritual or temporal, but often our prayers sound like the Christmas wish list of a young child. We may ask for a better job, release from suffering, and peace, all of which we are entitled to ask for, and much of which we will receive.

But when our prayers are answered, what do we do? We give thanks in private, because whose business is it what we have prayed for and received? But Jesus says prayers are answered only for one reason: so that His actions on our behalf will bring glory to the Father. Do we give God the glory when our prayers are answered, or do we keep it to ourselves?

Lord, You see to it that our prayers, big and small, are answered every day.
When they are, give us the courage to openly give You the credit for our success.

Maybe hate is too strong a word. Still, some days it seems that the world—or at least one person—is highly disappointed by how we turned out. We can't do anything right. And by the time the day is over, we're ready to call it quits and go to sleep.

> "If the world hates you, keep in mind that it hated me first."
> JOHN 15:18 NIV

There's no such thing as a new way of suffering, and you are not the first to feel hated, persecuted, or abandoned. When you feel that the whole world is against you, keep in mind that it first hated Jesus, God's only Son. And when He felt the hate of the world, Jesus just went on forgiving those who hated Him.

You are not alone. You have your spouse to lean on in times of trouble, as well as the One who was hated before you were even born.

Lord, thank You for giving me a loving companion to help me in days of trouble.
Thank You for showing us how to deal with those who treat us poorly.

_____THURSDAY_____

> "Now is your time of grief,
> but I will see you again
> and you will rejoice,
> and no one will take away your joy."
>
> JOHN 16:22 NIV

While grief comes in many forms, it is always related to some type of loss. A mother crying as she leaves her child at school on the first day of kindergarten is suffering from grief, even if she doesn't recognize the emotion. A soldier leaving his family behind, as well as those being left at home, will suffer grief. Even the act of moving to a new house or town, or having friends move away, will cause us real pain. The worst kind of grief, and the most lasting, is the pain we feel when someone we love dies.

A Christian family will suffer as much grief as any other family. Loss will hurt them just as deeply. The difference is, a Christian's grief is always tempered by hope. The loved one is still gone, but we have the hope of meeting again in heaven and experiencing permanent joy.

Father, when grief comes to us,
be with us in our suffering and remind us of the joy that will be ours forever.

You're married, supporting yourself and your family the best you can, and *still* your parents are giving you unsolicited advice! Will they never let you lead your own life?

Why in the world would you want them to do that? Consider that, aside from your spouse and God, they know you better than anyone and they always have your best interests at heart. Who else will love you no matter what you say or do?

Your parents' advice may not always be perfect, but at least it is given in love and with no strings attached. Besides, as time goes by, you may even see that Mom and Dad were more often right than wrong!

A fool despiseth
his father's instruction:
but he that regardeth reproof
is prudent.
PROVERBS 15:5 KJV

Father, when I refuse to listen to my parents' advice,
the only fool in the room is me.
Give me the sense at least to listen and consider what they say,
the way I do when my friends offer their advice.

> "The LORD your God
> will make you abound in
> all the work of your hand."
> DEUTERONOMY 30:9 NKJV

It's the depths of winter, the perfect time to try your hand at some home improvements! Of course, those with a talent or training in carpentry will tackle more ambitious projects than those who can barely handle a hammer. Still, there's something around the house for everyone to do, even if it involves painting the bathroom ceiling (you know no one ever looks up there, but you'll feel better when it's done). Working together on a project will be worth a few laughs and a joint sense of accomplishment, even if a professional could have done the job better. You may not be qualified to start knocking down walls or rewiring the house, but with a little advice from your home center, you can learn to stop that annoying faucet drip, change the faceplate on an outlet, or paint a dingy room.

Lord, neither of us has much experience in home improvement,
but we're willing to learn.
Help us keep our sense of humor when things don't turn out perfectly,
and use this time to bring us closer as a couple.

_____

_____

_____

_____

_____

_____

_____

_____

_____

Here are some projects that are easy to do and make for quick improvements:

1. Stencil a border around the top of a room's walls, or paste up a ready-made one.

2. Replace all the old, mismatched doorknobs in a room.

3. Change the character of a room by putting up new curtains or blinds.

4. Check to see if there is a good wood floor under the ratty wall-to-wall carpeting you hate, and pull up the rug if the floor is in good shape.

5. Hang a few plants by a sunny window and keep them alive until spring arrives.

6. Sand down and refinish a door, table, or floor.

7. Rent a rug-cleaning machine and return the rug to its original color.

8. Replace the old kitchen faucet with a shiny new one.

9. Put new handles on an old drawer.

10. Move the refrigerator and stove out from the wall and vacuum up everything living under there.

A fool's wrath is presently known:
but a prudent man covereth shame.
PROVERBS 12:16 KJV

No matter how much we love our partners, there are times when they upset us or even cause us shame. We are still two different people—sometimes very different—and what would not bother one in the least can cause the other to fly into a rage. It takes time to explore and define emotional boundaries, and to realize how far an argument can be carried before reason leaves the conversation and emotions take over.

Proverbs warns us to hold our tongues and not lash out at each other. Give your emotions time to subside; go for a drive or take a walk alone. Know that once you say the words you know will hurt your spouse the most, there is no taking them back, and the hurt you inflict could last for years.

Father, I know very well how to hurt my partner,
to find that one weak spot that is the tenderest and most vulnerable.
When I am feeling hurt and unloved,
give me the self-control not to say the words that will hurt the most.

'Tis the cold and flu season, and if one of you is sick, the other soon will be, too. Common, ordinary sickness is a trying experience for both the sick and the well. You never know a spouse until you have lived with a sick one. If you feel a sick person belongs in bed, your partner will feel the need to be right there, in the middle of things, spraying germs all over the house. If you believe in toughing it out, your partner will stay in bed and moan for three long days.

> "For I will restore health to you and heal you of your wounds," says the LORD.
> JEREMIAH 30:17 NKJV

Now is not the time to pick a fight, not when it will soon be you who is sneezing and in pain. We each have to do battle with sickness on our own terms, no matter what our mothers told us. So, stock up on whatever makes your partner feel better and pray for quick healing.

Father, give me patience through this season's illness.
Help me be a kind, caring spouse who thinks of the other, not of myself,
even when I'm sure he or she isn't handling sickness the proper way.

> "Are not my days few?
> Cease! Leave me alone."
> JOB 10:20 NKJV

Job had been more than patient with his friends, but now he wanted to be left alone in peace. Is your partner like Job when illness strikes? Some people want to curl up under a pile of blankets and just ride it out in peace and quiet. That's what works for them, as long as someone else remembers to check on them now and then and supply food and medicine. They don't want anyone hovering over them or cheering them up when they feel that there's absolutely nothing to be cheerful about.

You, the healthy one, are the one who must adjust. There's no point in keeping such a sufferer company, in reading the paper aloud, or in finding a good program on television. Your efforts will not be appreciated and you will only be amusing yourself—something better done in another room.

Father, I get lonely and miserable when my partner is sick
and refuses to be comforted by my company.
Help me not to take it personally.

Then there are the whiners, those who refuse to be sick alone. No bed rest for them. They will put on several layers of clothing and sit on the couch and moan. If you don't respond to the first little moans, they will most assuredly grow louder and become more frequent, until they begin to frighten pets and small children.

> Have mercy on me,
> O Lord, for I am weak.
> PSALM 6:2 NKJV

Such people need company, day and night. They want to be talked to, listened to, and hovered over. They want menu choices explained to them; they want their temperature taken and the doctor alerted. They want to play an active part in their own healing, often warming up soup at two in the morning or throwing your medicine schedule out of sync by taking some whenever they feel they need it. These people need watching, in other words!

Needless to say, you will be driven up the wall long before the patient gets well.

O Lord, my partner is sick again, and I'm not feeling too well myself.
Have mercy on us both, for we are weak.

Week 4

> I am weary with my groaning;
> all night I make my bed swim;
> I drench my couch with my tears.
>
> PSALM 6:6 NKJV

This person sounds really sick. He's depressed, sweating like a pig from a fever, and emotionally sensitive. You don't want to get too close to this one, but you'd better bundle him up and drive him to the doctor, just to be safe.

Being able to tell when your partner is really sick is something you want to learn as soon as possible. Many people try to hide the extent of their illness or downright refuse to be sick at all. The faster you learn to tell the difference between a head cold and some rampaging illness, the better. Symptoms will vary from person to person, but if you find yourself worrying more than usual about your patient, trust your instincts and get some help.

*Father, I would rather overreact and have the doctor laugh at me
than risk the chance of losing the person I love.
If I am not paying attention to serious symptoms,
please open my eyes and tell me what needs to be done.*

The end of the football season is upon us; the ultimate game of the year is about to be played. All over the United States, husbands will be glued to televisions through the pregame show, the game, the postgame show, and a whole raft of new and fascinating commercials. Wives have only two duties today: keep the food coming and prevent the children from standing between their fathers and the TV.

Bring out Samson to entertain us.
JUDGES 16:25 NIV

At least this time the athletes are not prisoners who will, at the end of the game, bring the marital roof down on all the spectators. You can thank the ingenuity of countless wives for that. Who do you think invented the Super Bowl Party? "If we lock them in a dark room with the TV," one woman said to another, "and keep them supplied with junk food, we can all have a good time out here. We will all be happy, and the game won't make us fight with our husbands."

So go ahead, bring out Samson to entertain us.

Lord, husbands and wives don't always enjoy the same things.
When our interests conflict, show us a compromise that will make both of us happy.

There is only one male activity this weekend, so adjust.

1. Give or attend a Super Bowl Party. (Remember, you don't have to watch the game.)

2. If no party is available, take the kids to a movie.

3. If no movie is suitable, go visit your parents.

4. If your parents are unavailable, go visit your husband's parents.

5. If none of the above is possible, sit next to your husband and watch the game. It may be more fun than you believed possible.

Remember when you were a child you prayed the same prayer every evening before going to sleep? "God bless Mommy and Daddy and. . . ." If you weren't ready to go to sleep yet, you could drag that list on forever. Now you may look back on that simple prayer and laugh at its innocence, but who can say that those prayers were not fervent or deny they could have made a difference in someone's life?

Confess your faults one to another, and pray one for another, that ye may be healed. The effectual fervent prayer of a righteous man availeth much.

JAMES 5:16 KJV

Do you pray as regularly for your spouse as you once did for your parents and other family members? Your world is certainly more complex, as are your prayers, but taking time to ask God to bless the one you love might be the most important thing you can do for your marriage.

Father, remind me that there is someone close to me who needs and deserves my prayers every day.

Be ye angry, and sin not:
let not the sun go down
upon your wrath.
EPHESIANS 4:26 KJV

There's nothing more depressing than a two-day argument. If you go to sleep angry, you toss and turn all night because you know you'll only wake up in the middle of the same old fight. It's depressing to start the day with both of you at the extreme edges of the same bed. True, not every disagreement can be settled in one day, but there is no need to go to bed upset and angry.

No matter what the issue, you do have other things you agree on. Before you go to sleep, talk about the children, an upcoming vacation, or something good that happened at work. Tell your spouse you love him or her, and agree to disagree for the time being. Sometimes this reconciliation will be easy, and sometimes it will seem forced and insincere, but either way you need to go to sleep at peace with each other.

Father, we share so much as a couple that it's foolish to let
a disagreement ruin the whole day.
When we are arguing, remind us how much we love each other
and give us the strength to make peace.

_____
_____
_____
_____
_____
_____
_____
_____
_____
_____
_____
_____

Mutual respect is the foundation of a good marriage. Two different people may have legitimate opposing views on any subject, from how to handle money to which football team to support. Of importance is not the issue but how you treat each other.

> Let every one of you in particular so love his wife even as himself; and the wife see that she reverence her husband.
> EPHESIANS 5:33 KJV

The wife of Ephesians 5:33 is not being told to worship her husband and leave all the decisions to him. Only God deserves to be worshiped; only God never makes mistakes. She is told to respect her husband and give his views a fair, loving hearing. The husband is told to love his wife at least as much as he loves himself. That means he must respect her and give her views the same fair and loving hearing he expects for himself.

Don't fall into the "I'm in charge here" trap. You need each other's viewpoints to handle successfully the troubles that will come your way.

Father, You are in charge of our marriage.
You gave us each other as a gift of happiness.
Don't let our egos destroy that happiness.

Week 5

> So in everything,
> do to others what you would
> have them do to you,
> for this sums up
> the Law and the Prophets.
> MATTHEW 7:12 NIV

Treat someone badly and you can expect he'll return the favor. Often he won't stop a second before retaliating. Treat a person well and you may have earned yourself a lifelong friend. It's a trait of human nature to give as good as we get.

The truth of the Golden Rule works for us or against us in marriage. Even the most devoted spouse gets fed up with continual bad treatment, but few can resist someone who treats them with respect and consideration.

When your wife has a brutal workday and wants to order takeout food, do you dump on her about family finances, or do you offer to make dinner instead? When your husband doesn't feel like driving, do you offer to take the wheel?

Treating your spouse with consideration builds up your marriage and the friendship it's founded on. Following the Golden Rule could lead you to a golden anniversary.

Lord, we want to treat each other well for a lifetime, not just occasionally.
Give us the grace to treat each other well every day.

_____

_____

_____

_____

_____

_____

_____

_____

_____

_____

"He has all the tact of a water buffalo." "She's awful in the kitchen. I have to do all the cooking or the kids would go hungry." What you say about your spouse tells a lot about your marriage—and the kind of husband or wife you are. Has your marriage united a pair of serpents, with sharp, poisonous tongues?

> They make their tongues as sharp as a serpent's; the poison of vipers is on their lips.
> PSALM 140:3 NIV

In the happiest of marriages, husband and wife have learned to dull that tongue or just bite it when the news is bad. Instead happily married couples report the best about their spouses: his strengths, her talents, and the good things that are going on in their lives. Bad things may be mentioned, but they are dealt with in private, between two people who love each other and want the best for their marriage.

If you have a disagreement with your spouse, speak up, but not to your mother, friend, or coworker. Talk it out with your spouse instead of spreading poison through a family, church, or workplace. Tame that serpent before it poisons your life.

Thank You, Lord, that Satan's poison doesn't have to destroy our marriage.
Dull our tongues with kindness every day.

> If you forgive anyone,
> I also forgive him.
> And what I have forgiven. . .
> I have forgiven in the sight of
> Christ for your sake.
> 2 CORINTHIANS 2:10 NIV

Ever had a disagreement with your spouse and gone straight with the tale to your sister or mother? The results of that mistake were probably pretty nasty, a week, month, or year later. You settled the problem with your spouse, forgave each other, and it was all over between you. But if you shared that news with your family member, she probably had a hard time letting go of the shared anger.

When someone hurts the people we love, it's easy to hang on to resentment or start a family battle. It's hard to make peace again. Paul knew that when he described his forgive-and-forget attitude to the Corinthians.

Just in case your family isn't as spiritually mature as Paul, why not save them from sin? Don't rush off to share intimate arguments you only need to share with your spouse. Only two of you need to forgive and forget.

We don't want to start family battles, Lord.
Help us forgive and forget quickly—
before we open our mouths to others.

_____

_____

_____

_____

_____

_____

_____

_____

_____

_____

_____

_____

_____

How have you been speaking to your spouse, and what words have you used to describe your loved one to others? Today keep track of the things you say. How many are positive? Negative?

Ask yourself why you speak the way you do. Are you newlyweds so much in love that you can't help telling others? Or have you been married for years and still find your romance overflowing to others? What can you do to keep that love alive?

If speaking kind words is hard, take a look at what makes it difficult. Are hidden or yet unidentified hurts making you sabotage your spouse? Be honest with yourselves, so you can identify those hurts and begin to work them out with prayer, communication, and possibly advice from a wise counselor.

If you occasionally say harsh words to your spouse, what causes that? Does one issue in particular always spark unkind words? If so, identify it and begin to make the changes that will return kindness to your marriage.

> For there is not a word
> on my tongue, but behold, O LORD,
> You know it altogether.
> PSALM 139:4 NKJV

The married couple doesn't exist that hasn't exchanged words that shouldn't have been spoken. Occasionally we all open our mouths and cause distress. The moment we see the hurt those words caused, we may blurt out, "I'm sorry, I didn't mean that." Yet we writhe under the knowledge that words don't erase the pain.

Nothing, not even harsh words, are beyond God's knowledge and forgiveness. So why doesn't God stop us in midsentence? Couldn't He keep us from such sin?

Of course God could. But then the sinful attitudes and thoughts we harbor inside would remain a mystery. We'd never understand the hidden frustrations that work on our innermost parts.

When we let our mouths flap, we see ourselves as we really are—believers with rough spots. As God refines those rough spots in our love for Him, our mates can see a new love shine. Then our marriages truly reflect how we feel about the greatest Lover.

Lord God, thank You that no harsh words of ours can destroy Your love for us.
Make our lives reflect that love.

_____
_____
_____
_____
_____
_____
_____
_____
_____
_____
_____

Your spouse hurt you deeply. Whether words darted into your soul or an action offended you, your heart aches.

> And forgive us our debts, as we forgive our debtors.
> MATTHEW 6:12 KJV

What do you do? Holding a grudge may seem okay for a while, but where does it get you? Giving the silent treatment or needling your spouse only ruins communication and eventually destroys a marriage.

Maybe you need to wrestle with that pain. Take the time to understand why your husband or wife caused you anguish. But dwelling on the wrong won't ease the situation. Sooner or later—and the sooner, the better—you need to forgive that injury.

Accept that your spouse is human, makes mistakes, and falls victim to sin. Understand how much both of you need God's forgiveness and that you need to mirror His mercy in your married life.

Forgiveness isn't a one-way street. Tomorrow you may do something thoughtless and be looking for the same "no strings attached" pardon. You'll be glad it's there.

Lord God, thank You for not holding a grudge against us for our sin.
Help us forgive as You have forgiven us.

> If anyone considers himself religious and yet does not keep a tight rein on his tongue, he deceives himself and his religion is worthless.
>
> JAMES 1:26 NIV

Have you ever experienced "word failure"? You spoke words that were "good for" your spouse. After all, shouldn't he know what the congregation is saying about him? Shouldn't she know that people don't like it when she acts a certain way? You meant to be helpful, but your words simply brought you both anguish.

Your little sermon probably showed more about you than your spouse. That well-meant lecture fell short of God's grace and mercy, and instantly your faith was transformed into false religion.

Our "word failures" unexpectedly show up our "heart failures" toward God. Though we preach sermons, if our hearts haven't checked with God before our mouths open, we're in trouble.

Holding our tongues and praying, or seeking a better time and speaking gentle words, might have helped.

Lord, we want to serve each other in love, not correct each other with pain.
Keep our hearts (and mouths) in Your love.

Sometimes we see another's flaws so clearly. *Why can't she see that?* we may ask. *What will it take to get through to him?* we wonder silently.

Focus on that sin or weak spot and soon all you'll see are your spouse's flaws. All the good things can be shoved to the side. If you don't watch out, your mate can become one big blemish.

> "Therefore be merciful,
> just as your Father also is merciful.
> Judge not, and you shall not be judged.
> Condemn not,
> and you shall not be condemned.
> Forgive, and you will be forgiven."
>
> LUKE 6:36–37 NKJV

Instead, focus on forgiveness and encouragement to turn that relationship around. Rather than remaking your spouse in *your* image of what he or she should be, follow in God's footsteps, offering mercy that encourages spiritual growth and maturity. Let compassion replace the judgment and condemnation. Soon you'll find yourself with an appreciative spouse, and not one who can't wait to pick out your flaws.

Since we all sin, let the mercy flow freely.

Thank You, Lord, for showing us what mercy looks like.
Help us ask for forgiveness and give it freely.

God forgives us for sins great and small. Nothing is too large or inconsequential for His mercy.

Because the price He paid for that mercy was His only Son, Jesus, God takes forgiveness seriously. He doesn't see forgiveness as something to sweep under the rug. He expects those who have been forgiven to be willing to change their lifestyles.

> Therefore,
> since Christ suffered in his body,
> arm yourselves also with the same attitude,
> because he who has suffered
> in his body is done with sin.
> As a result, he does not live the rest of
> his earthly life for evil human desires,
> but rather for the will of God.
>
> 1 PETER 4:1–2 NIV

Those changes should influence our marriages, too. Instead of making our spouses suffer for our selfishness, we should become increasingly sensitive to our mates. When we wrong each other, we ought to ask for and offer forgiveness as quickly as possible. Our evil desires will decline as our godly goals increase.

Can you imagine a more "perfect" marriage than being wed to a spouse like that?

*Lord Jesus, You suffered to bring us freedom from sin;
help us to live to know and do Your will each day.*

_____

_____

_____

_____

_____

_____

_____

_____

_____

_____

_____

_____

When you were first dating, you probably wondered if your mate-to-be really liked you. Could this wonderful person be interested in *you?*

> If thou, LORD,
> shouldest mark iniquities,
> O Lord, who shall stand?
> But there is forgiveness with thee,
> that thou mayest be feared.
> PSALM 130:3–4 KJV

Sometimes we think that way about God, too. *Could a holy God care for me enough to forgive my sin?*

None of us can make God like us more or less. As the Holy One, He knows we are far from His standards. Yet He chooses to love us with an overwhelming love that, in earthly terms, costs more than we are worth.

If we're honest with ourselves, at times we also cost more than we're worth to our spouses. Sin can make us hard to live with. If our spouses started chalking up our iniquities, we'd be in for a short marriage.

A marriage that lasts recognizes frailties and uses God's forgiveness to erase the chalkboard daily. After all, if we kept track on God's terms, who would stand?

Thank You, Lord, for giving us the ability to forgive.
Let our hands be quick to pick up Your eraser.

Week 6

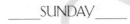

Forgiveness isn't just a concept to understand but one that should be active in our lives. Put forgiveness into your lives this weekend by taking these actions.

1. Together, spend time in prayer about forgiveness. Ask God if there are any unforgiven sins that harm your relationship with each other. Then discuss some of these issues, remembering to be sensitive to each other's hurts. If an issue becomes touchy, you may need to return to prayer or take a break.

2. Is there a family member or friend whom you need to forgive (or who needs to forgive you)? Pray about that relationship and make plans to heal the rift. (If it's a long-term hurt, consider contacting others—your pastor, a church leader, or another counselor—for special wisdom.)

3. When you have sought forgiveness, remember to thank God for the healing that has taken place. If there are still some sore spots, continue to pray for them regularly.

_____

Are you waiting for your mate to become perfect before you show your love? If so, you'll wait till eternity. People don't become perfect, apart from Jesus' earthly transformation, and as long as we're in this sin-torn world, none of us reaches absolute godly perfection.

> But God demonstrates
> His own love toward us,
> in that while we were still sinners,
> Christ died for us.
> ROMANS 5:8 NKJV

Like God, who loved us even when we had no thought of Him, we must love our spouses *before* they become perfect. We need to encourage them to seek God's will and overcome flaws, but we need to love them during the process. A promise of "I'll love you when you attain this," or "I'll accept you when you overcome such-and-such a sin," is an empty one.

The more we love, the more "perfect" Mr. or Mrs. Right becomes. Suddenly those flaws don't seem so large. The things our spouses do well and the spiritual maturity they have attained loom larger than the faults we once "corrected."

Help us love each other unconditionally, Lord, as You have loved us.
We want to focus on the strengths You've given each of us and overcome the flaws.

> A merry heart does good,
> like medicine,
> but a broken spirit dries the bones.
> PROVERBS 17:22 NKJV

Bad things happen in life: Sorrow comes when we lose a loved one; our finances may reduce drastically; a child may disappoint us. We often can't control situations, and we can't make wiser choices for others.

What we can decide is what will break our spirits. Will the loss of a job, which may someday be replaced, make us lose faith? Will challenges with a child make us so negative that we also harm our marriage?

Want to feel bad? Just meditate on all those "woe is me" thoughts. Soon you'll not only feel depressed, but your body will catch up to your thinking and you'll have aches and pains to spare.

Keeping your mind on the most positive things you can contemplate is like taking a wonder drug—in other words, good medicine—that puts zip back into your step.

The best medicine or dried-up bones can testify to your faith. Which will it be?

Sometimes, Lord, we can't see beyond one painful hour.
Please help us to keep our hearts cheerful through Your love.

Anyone who thinks God has no romance in His makeup is dead wrong. It only takes a peek at the Song of Solomon to see that God invented romance. This short, powerful book describes the passionate outpouring of God's emotions on those who believe in Him.

> Your love is
> more delightful than wine.
> SONG OF SOLOMON 1:2 NIV

Though it describes the relationship between God and His people, the Song of Solomon has much to say to husbands and wives. God designed marriage to be a delightful experience shared by a man and woman. The power of wedded bliss to intoxicate goes far beyond wine yet lacks wine's harmful properties.

There's no church holiday for romantic love, but Valentine's Day is a good time to remember how much your spouse means to you and to appreciate the love God has given you.

Be intoxicated with each other, without even taking a sip of wine!

Thank You, Father God, for showing us the joy of married love.
Help us to take time today to express the depth of emotion that we share.

_____THURSDAY_____

> A kindhearted woman
> gains respect,
> but ruthless men gain only wealth.
> PROVERBS 11:16 NIV

In the workplace you may have run into one of those hard-hitting types who has a bundle of money but is despised by everyone. He thinks no one can see through his machinations, but most know he can't be trusted.

Maybe his wife is a kind, gentle soul whom everyone loves. Though her husband hasn't a clue, the only reason he gets invited anywhere socially is because people respect her enough to be too embarrassed not to let him tag along.

In this world he may seem like the big cheese because he owns a company, a yacht, and real estate. But in heaven people may be surprised to find that she has a place of honor, while he has disappeared into insignificance.

Today, are you living for heaven or only to acquire earthly possessions?

Keep us mindful of Your truth, Father God, as we live from day to day.
Let our bank account be of service to You instead of a sign of our disobedience.

Gomer, the prophet Hosea's wife, had fallen into serious sin by seeking the affections of other men. So God made a promise to Hosea. Life wouldn't turn out the way Gomer had expected, and trouble would make her return to Hosea.

> Therefore I will block her path with thornbushes; I will wall her in so that she cannot find her way.
> HOSEA 2:6 NIV

Even though we have been faithful, we might empathize with Gomer. There we are, living each day, everything organized and neat, when *wham!* life starts falling apart. Suddenly our spouses seem about a mile away, and troubles multiply. While things are going along fine, we can't see that we begin to depend on ourselves, forget the needs of our mates, and leave less and less time in our days for God.

Sometimes we all need "thornbushes" to get us right with our mates and Maker. When the stickers prick our skin, we recognize how much we need God—and our spouses—and start reorganizing our lives to reflect that.

God can move thornbushes, not just mountains!

Thank You, Lord, for bringing thornbushes into our lives,
to show us when we're stuck.
Draw us closer to You, and to each other,
before we reach those bushes.

> He who did not spare His own Son,
> but delivered Him up for us all,
> how shall He not with Him
> also freely give us all things?
> ROMANS 8:32 NKJV

To love is to give. If someone says, "I love you," but won't help you out or give in other ways, chances are that person isn't really loving. Together, you won't have much of a relationship.

God not only gives to us, He gives extravagantly. He offered up His Son, the dearest thing He had to give. Anything else seems small in comparison. And God keeps on giving good gifts—and only good gifts—all the time.

To have a happy marital relationship also means giving: time, effort, forgiveness, and that special every-morning kiss. It also means occasionally giving physical gifts: a how-to video he's wanted for a long time, or a rose to tell her she's special. Whether it's a helping hand or a wrapped-up package, each gift shows your spouse you know what he or she needs and that you care for that need.

What need can you fill for your spouse today?

*Father God, thank You for loving us so much that You gave us just what we needed—
Your Son, Jesus. We want to show love to each other by giving good gifts, too.*

_____

_____

_____

_____

_____

_____

_____

_____

_____

_____

_____

_____

_____

_____

_____

_____

_____

_____

How do you show your love? How does your mate like to be shown love? Are the two the same? Take turns talking about the things you like that your mate does for you and the ways your husband or wife could improve. What "gifts" of time and consideration do you each need? What physical gifts make you the happiest?

Remember to speak gently to each other. Don't turn this into a criticism fest, but do share the good and the less than perfect. Each of you needs to have a fair say and some time to discuss what is said.

If you can't afford physical gifts right now, start a "wish book" and begin to set goals that will help you earn the money to satisfy at least a few moderate wishes. Update your book as you can afford those gifts so your spouse will always have ideas for birthday or Christmas gifts.

_____ MONDAY _____

> A perverse man
> stirs up dissension,
> and a gossip
> separates close friends.
> PROVERBS 16:28 NIV

Family life can be challenging, especially if you're dealing with in-laws.

You married a wonderful person. On your wedding day you had visions of blue skies for the rest of your life. Obviously you weren't looking at your new spouse's Uncle Willie or Aunt Jane.

What you say and do around your mate's family influences how they feel about you. Argue with Uncle Willie, just for fun, and your mate won't have fun the next time she phones Aunt Jane. Gossip about Jane's after-church pastimes, and you'll hear about it after church *next* Sunday.

Such situations are avoidable. Treat your spouse's relatives with respect, even if you can't agree with everything they do, and usually you'll be able to win them over. But more than anything, treat your spouse respectfully. They'll be relieved to see that your good marriage makes your mate happy.

Thank You, Lord, for my mate's family, even if we don't always agree.
After all, I wouldn't have such a great spouse if it weren't for that family.

Before you marry you can do as you please, spiritually and in other ways. But once you commit to your spouse, you have to take that person into consideration. Paul was just pointing out the obvious—someone with his challenging ministry in the face of persecution had to choose between God and marriage.

> But a married man is concerned about the affairs of this world—how he can please his wife. . . . But a married woman is concerned about the affairs of this world—how she can please her husband.
>
> 1 CORINTHIANS 7:33–34 NIV

If you think you can spend all your time at work or on a ministry, think again. It isn't fair to give your spouse only the late-night hours when you're wiped out from a hectic day. You won't communicate clearly under those conditions, and arguments are likely to come more often and fiercely.

Married couples need time together, uninterrupted by children, work, or family chores. Whether it's regular date nights or a few hours set aside for morning devotions and talk, schedule time to share. Your spouse will be pleased to no end.

Lord, we often lose track of our need to spend time together without distractions.
Help us to please each other, and not just our bosses.

**The contentions of a wife
are a continual dripping.**
PROVERBS 19:13 NKJV

Drip, drip, drip, what an irritating sound! You'd do almost anything to stop it. Maybe that's why so many use the "driplike" technique of nagging to try to get their way.

But nagging isn't a productive way to deal with problems. It just irritates one's spouse and shows the nagger's foolishness. After a while the nagged mate just ignores the scolding and goes his or her own way.

Nagging can serve a useful purpose, though, if both spouses treat it as a warning signal. When your spouse keeps mentioning the same concern or situation, it's time to wake up and realize that you need to deal with something here.

Maybe you need to call in a plumber or carpenter to fix something in the house, or maybe you need to discuss an aspect of your marriage. Whatever it is, stop that leak before it floats your marriage off its foundations.

*Lord, we don't want to turn into a pair of naggers.
Give us the wisdom to solve our problems before they float us away.*

_____

_____

_____

_____

_____

_____

_____

_____

_____

_____

_____

_____

The Bible doesn't have too many examples of awful spouses, but Job's wife is one. Her husband faced the biggest trial of his life and all she could say was "Curse God and die!" *Get a way out of it, even at the cost of your integrity* was her message. *God doesn't matter anymore—look at the pain you're in!* In one "swoosh" she pulled out from under Job his only potential human support and comfort.

> His wife said to him,
> "Are you still
> holding on to your integrity?
> Curse God and die!"
> JOB 2:9 NIV

Is your spouse is facing a trial? Don't dump a negative message on your mate. Instead, lift him or her up with encouragement and love.

Don't influence your mate to sin but to stand firm for God. Remind your spouse that God still provides love and support for the hard times. There's nothing the two of you can't get through, if you lean on God.

We don't want to emulate Mrs. Job, Lord.
Instead we want to be faithful to You, even when we face trials.
Help us to look for Your blessing in every circumstance.

_____FRIDAY_____

> Catch us the foxes,
> the little foxes that spoil the vines,
> for our vines have tender grapes.
> SONG OF SOLOMON 2:15 NKJV

Often it isn't big things that make a marriage uncomfortable. Rather, it's the little, picky problems that may disturb an otherwise happy relationship. Just a touch of an unforgiving attitude here or a lack of consideration there can make you wake up grumpy in the morning and carry an unsettled feeling through the day. You bark at coworkers and your spouse, and don't even realize why.

Those small annoyances are like little foxes plundering the grapes in the vineyard. They may not ruin the vines, but they sure impact the crop. Just as the hardworking farmer begins to wonder if he's in the business of feeding foxes or growing grapes, you start wondering who escaped with the joy that once flooded your marriage.

To make sure your marriage goes well, catch the foxes of bitterness, lack of forgiveness, and irritation before they ruin your joy.

Lord God, we don't want a loveless marriage that gives no testimony to You.
We want to keep the troubles in our relationship small by
coming to You with even the small sins.

_____

_____

_____

_____

_____

_____

_____

_____

_____

_____

_____

_____

_____

_____

_____

_____

_____

_____

_____

_____

_____

_____

_____

Two become one because they love each other. They have visions of a shared life that will uplift them both. Then that unloving relative comes along with criticism and doubts. "I told you he'll never amount to much." "What interest have we in one of *her* kind?"

> "For if you love those who love you, what reward have you? Do not even the tax collectors do the same?"
> MATTHEW 5:46 NKJV

Or a thousand other objections.

God understands the pain and the sin that harm a relationship, but His solution, to our minds, seems an odd one. He doesn't recommend that we avoid the bitter relative but that we love that person, even if he or she seems incredibly unlovable and the return seems meager.

After all, even the most immoral people can love someone who loves them, but praying for someone who has hurt you and keeping up as much of a relationship as possible—that takes Christian character.

Lord, unloving people can take the shine out of our days.
Help us to love them as much as they let us,
and keep us praying until love changes hearts.

Families can have a huge impact on your relationship, but unless you spend time with them, you're unlikely to become very close. Setting aside time for your larger family is important.

If possible, invite your in-laws for dinner one night simply to spend time together. Newlyweds can learn more about family members, and those who have been married for years can enjoy each other. If your family is not nearby, make plans for a short, shared vacation, invite them to visit you, if you can, or write a letter that shares some of your life.

If any difference of opinion has separated you, pray before you invite those family members. Perhaps this will be a good chance to come to an understanding. If that's not possible, make the time enjoyable and pray for an increase in understanding.

Whether you need money to pay the bills or answers on how to deal with balky teenagers, you've probably prayed a "Help, quick!" prayer to God. Everyone has those moments when nothing on earth, not even our much-loved spouses, seems to answer the need. Only God is big enough for this trouble.

> But I am poor and needy;
> make haste to me, O God!
> You are my help and my deliverer;
> O LORD, do not delay.
> PSALM 70:5 NKJV

There's no weakness in coming to God when we need help. It isn't wrong to ask for assistance in our marriage or relationships or even for our earthly needs. David knew that when he asked God not to let his enemies kill him. The soon-to-be king knew God wanted to hear about all his troubles.

God loves to hear all our prayers, even the ones that begin "Help, quick!" When we see an out-of-control SUV hurtling down the road toward us, when we enter a crowded emergency room with a seriously ill loved one, or when we just don't know what to say in response to someone's critical words, God is only a prayer away.

Whenever we need deliverance, He's there to care. We just need to be humble enough to ask.

Thank You, Father God, that You hear our every prayer.
Give us humble hearts to ask for our every need.

> "Therefore
> what God has joined together,
> let not man separate."
> MARK 10:9 NKJV

You think you have a happy marriage—until a friend starts to criticize your spouse. Suddenly you wonder if you've made the right choice, if you're getting the best out of life, or if you should have married someone more "spiritual."

When you feel that way, you've experienced a separation tactic Satan often uses on the unwary. If he can get another person between you and your spouse, whispering in your ear, he can take the *lock* out of *wedlock*.

Don't second-guess your decision to marry. Remember your marriage vows. You promised God that you would stay with this person for a lifetime, not until you tired of marriage or came to the sudden discovery that you hadn't married a "perfect" someone. Marriage isn't about *your* perfection or your spouse's; it's a covenant based on *God's* perfection and His plan for both of you.

Lord, we don't want to be separated by anyone.
Keep us tight together in You.

_____

_____

_____

_____

_____

_____

_____

_____

_____

_____

_____

The disciples didn't feel comfortable knowing a person might have to stick with a marriage that didn't appear to have a terrific future. Not much has changed since the first century.

> And in the house his disciples asked him again of the same matter. And he saith unto them, Whosoever shall put away his wife, and marry another, committeth adultery against her.
>
> MARK 10:10–11 KJV

Few of us like to close out divorce. We'd rather think there's a "back door" we can sneak out if things get rough. Our sin nature hates unrestricted commitment.

Try to stick to marital responsibilities solely under your own power and you *will* look for a back door, because any sin-filled person has a tough time remaining faithful. But you slam that back door and lock it when you allow God free rein in your marriage. Though you can't ignore marital problems, thinking they'll solve themselves, you can overcome them, with God's strength. When His Spirit fills your marriage, you'll avoid some troubles. Instead of despairing, you grow through the trials. As you conform to His likeness, your lives are transformed, and marriage becomes better.

And *that's* a terrific future.

Lord Jesus, Your words may not be easy to accept,
but we know You will help us follow them.
Fill us with Your Spirit so we can be conformed to Your likeness.

> Teach us to number
> our days aright,
> that we may gain
> a heart of wisdom.
> PSALM 90:12 NIV

On leap year you get an "extra" day—but how will you use it? Will it be a banner day in your marriage, or one you wish you could forget? Will you act as if you'll live forever and need not keep track of your time, or will you use it wisely?

When it comes to the length of your life, you don't get "extra" days. God already has in mind how many years you'll live and how many days will be in each one. You can't change that.

What you can change is how wisely you use your time.

Take this day and use it for God. Bless your spouse and family. Make wise choices. Only then will you have properly numbered the day.

Help us to use each day wisely, Lord, to serve You and others.

_____ THURSDAY _____

What qualities did you see in your partner that made you decide, *This is the one*? Was it passion or politeness? wealth or wisdom? success or steadfastness? Although the qualities in the verse on the right seem very different from those admired by our culture, they are probably close to what your mother told you to look for in a mate. Kindness, truthfulness, faithfulness, patience, and joyfulness—all the attributes of a good Christian—make for a good spouse.

> What is desired in a man is kindness, and a poor man is better than a liar.
> PROVERBS 19:22 NKJV

Don't let the media convince you that there is something missing in your partner because she's a little overweight or he is developing a bald spot on the top of his head. On those days when your spouse is obviously less than perfect, remember why you fell in love in the first place.

Father, neither of us is perfect by today's standards.
But it was Your standards that attracted us to each other
and will keep us together for the rest of our lives.

> But,
> speaking the truth in love. . . .
> EPHESIANS 4:15 NKJV

There are two ways to speak the truth: in love and not in love. Some couples vow never to keep the truth from each other, no matter what. Others are more foresighted, realizing that the brutal truth is not always what people want or need to hear.

"How do I look in this dress?" has only one acceptable answer: "You look absolutely wonderful!"

"Am I going bald?" does not deserve an absolutely truthful answer either. "You're more handsome than ever" will do nicely.

It's not that you are lying when you sidestep this type of question. Your husband does think you look wonderful, and you do think he's more handsome than ever. You just didn't answer the question the way it was posed. The point is, you are speaking the truth—in love.

Father, we realize that the truth is the best answer
but not when it would hurt the one we love.
Help us to speak the truth with love.

A couple made up of two strong personalities is sure to have an interesting life together, to say the least. There will be more bumps in their marriage than for two more laid-back mates. This is not in itself a problem as long as both know how to handle disagreements in a loving manner.

> Not rendering evil for evil, or railing for railing: but contrariwise blessing; knowing that ye are thereunto called, that ye should inherit a blessing.
> 1 PETER 3:9 KJV

Strong-willed people attack problems with determination, overcome them, and then go on to the next task. What may at first seem to be a weakness in their relationship can turn out to be a blessing.

Father, two strong people do not have to pull in opposite directions.
When they pull together, with Your help, they can move mountains.
Remind us of that the next time we disagree.

This weekend take an inventory of your gifts and abilities. Each of you should make your own personal list, then share them for a few laughs. Be specific and truthful. If you can handle a hammer but not a saw, don't write down that you're a good carpenter. Do say, though, that you can hang any picture that needs hanging. Are you a good driver, or great at handling family finances? Can you get the kids to bed faster than your spouse, or bake a cherry pie? Maybe your talents are just waiting to turn an unkempt patch of weeds into a thriving vegetable garden. Whatever your skills, have fun with your own personal inventory and don't be afraid to boast a little.

_____MONDAY_____

_____

_____

_____

_____

_____

_____

_____

_____

_____

_____

_____

We all have friends like that, so well spoken and kind on the surface, yet so eager to strike as soon as our backs are turned. Whether we meet them at work or in our neighborhood, they can hurt us with their treachery.

> The words of his mouth
> were smoother than butter,
> but war was in his heart;
> his words were softer than oil,
> yet they were drawn swords.
> PSALM 55:21 NKJV

Fortunately, a couple can always watch each other's back. Do you have a friend that your spouse doesn't like or trust? One who seems so friendly when you're all together but dumps on your spouse as soon as the two of you are alone? If you are not mature enough to avoid friends like this, you should listen to your spouse when he or she warns you about this person. Someday that friend may turn on you, too.

Lord, our evaluation of our friends is not always accurate.
Thank You for giving us someone who always has our best interests at heart,
and make us willing to consider the advice our spouse offers.

> Live joyfully with the wife
> whom thou lovest.
> ECCLESIASTES 9:9 KJV

A young couple committed to each other often finds marriage to be a lot of work. The first few years are a time of adjustment and compromise, a time to settle the basic issues. Then you may decide to have children, with all the work that entails. As your family grows, so do your bills, and you work harder and longer.

Don't let all the issues and the children and the stress destroy the joy that comes with marriage. Never be too busy to enjoy quiet times with your spouse, to laugh or play like the children you once were together. Keep your relationship young and happy. In time, your children will grow up and leave, and once again it will be just the two of you. Will you find that you and your spouse are strangers, or will you greet that time of your life with joy? It all depends on what you do now.

Father, remind us how to play, and how to enjoy being with each other.
Help us remain best friends and lovers throughout our lives.

_____
_____
_____
_____
_____
_____
_____
_____
_____
_____
_____
_____
_____

Do you believe Jesus is your Savior? Do you believe God has the power to do anything He wants? Do you believe He loves you and wants only the best for you? Do you believe He answers the prayers of those who believe?

> "If you have faith and do not doubt whatever things you ask in prayer, believing, you will receive."
> MATTHEW 21:21–22 NKJV

If you have answered all of the above in the affirmative, you have already seen the effectiveness of prayer. Perhaps some of your prayers have been answered so fast it frightened you. Others you can see becoming answered one step at a time. Still others have not yet been answered, or were answered in ways you cannot see or understand. But, one way or another, your prayers are being heard and answered, because you believe.

Father, we know You answer our prayers every day,
but we don't always see the results or understand Your answers.
Whatever Your answer, we have faith that it will be exactly what we need.

_____THURSDAY_____

> Thou hast put gladness
> in my heart.
> PSALM 4:7 KJV

Somewhere, sometime, a friend or relative has probably asked you, "What do you see in that person?"

You can go to great lengths to answer the question, ticking off one point after another until your questioner caves in and backs off. Or you can become angry and lash out in reply, which will make you feel better but doesn't answer the question.

The next time someone asks such a tactless question, avoid both explanation and anger by quietly saying, "She [He] makes me happy." Even the most critical of people will admit (at least in their hearts) that there is no comeback to that answer.

Lord, You have given us each other because You knew we would make each other happy.
In an unhappy world, that is one of the greatest gifts of all.

The dictionary defines *covetousness* as "marked by inordinate desire for wealth or possessions or for another's possessions." *Inordinate* means "exceeding reasonable limits." So covetousness is basically an unreasonable desire for something you don't have but others may. Not a healthy state of mind.

> Let your conversation be without covetousness; and be content with such things as ye have.
> HEBREWS 13:5 KJV

The Bible does not say you should refrain from wanting a better life for yourself. Doing that would be as abnormal as coveting. What God's Word does say is that until you achieve your desires, you should be content with what you have and not waste time envying others. You can sit in front of the TV all day, coveting the newest and the best, or you can get out and earn what you want.

Father, we know You want the best for us,
but the best for us is not necessarily what is best for our neighbors.
Keep us from covetousness but not from hope.

SATURDAY

> But every man hath his
> proper gift of God,
> one after this manner,
> and another after that.
> 1 CORINTHIANS 7:7 KJV

Does your spouse deglaze or defrost? Is he a handyman or hopeless with a hammer? Do you ever wonder how the pioneers learned to do all they did to survive? Well, some of them were probably pretty bad at sewing (or sowing), and a lot of families must have eaten terrible pies and ridden in broken-down carriages.

When you are feeling especially inept at some household chore—or your spouse can't handle something your parents could—it's best to laugh it off and hire some help. We all have our own particular strengths, and Grandpa, who seems able to do everything, still can't check his own e-mail.

Father, thank You for the gifts we do have between us.
They may not be the same gifts other generations had,
but all of them are blessings.

No matter what the weather is like this weekend, spring is on its way. Why not give it a hand and banish cabin fever at the same time? If the ground has defrosted and dried enough, begin digging your garden and adding nutrients. You may even be able to plant peas by now. If not, start some seeds indoors or rake the leaves out of the flowerbeds. Perennials would love a good bed of mulch put down to warm their roots and keep weeds from popping up as the soil warms. If you have no outdoor space for gardening, buy some new houseplants or revive the ones you already have. Get your hands dirty and take part in the miracle of spring.

> Listen, my son,
> to your father's instruction
> and do not forsake
> your mother's teaching.
> PROVERBS 1:8 NIV

You have been listening to your father and mother all your life, but now you are half of a couple, dedicated to making your relationship last and grow. There will be times when your spouse must come first, when you will have to put his or her wishes ahead of those of your parents. Wise parents understand this and don't take it personally when you put your spouse first, but sometimes they still need to put in their two cents' worth.

How do you handle this type of conflict? Very carefully! Your parents must accept that you are no longer just their child but also a husband or wife and that your spouse's wishes must take first place in your decisions. At the same time, you must accept that your parents still have a lot they can teach you and you owe them your respect. Welcome their input whenever possible, thank them for their love and care, and then do what you have to do. They'll understand.

Father, give us the love and tactfulness we need in situations like this so no one is hurt or disappointed and we all remain "family."

If you have children, you can appreciate this verse. It takes two people to put three children to bed with no tears on anyone's part. Once they outnumber you, you need all the help you can get. The same holds true in other endeavors. Balancing the checkbook is difficult if one of you throws away those ATM slips, but working together you can develop a system that will handle the problem.

> Two are better than one,
> because they have a good return
> for their work:
> If one falls down,
> his friend can help him up.
> ECCLESIASTES 4:9–10 NIV

In spiritual matters, two individuals with differing talents but one faith can accomplish much for the church. One may be a fearless witness while the other is an effective prayer warrior. One loves to teach Sunday school, while the other is a bear in the thrift shop. Whatever you do in life, do it as a team made up of two different people. Watch your accomplishments pile up, your fears blow away, and your joy abound.

Father, thank You for my best friend and partner,
who brings out the best in me and supports me when I stumble.

> It is better to trust in the LORD
> than to put confidence in man.
> It is better to trust in the LORD
> than to put confidence in princes.
> PSALM 118:8–9 NKJV

Two of the most dangerous words in the English language are "trust me." Whoever says this is asking you to suspend your natural intelligence and avoid asking the hard questions. Whoever says this may be placing you in financial or personal danger, or even pitting you against your spouse. If you're in the military, you don't have much choice in the matter. Otherwise, following someone blindly is an act of stupidity, whether you're being asked to trust a used car salesman or a politician.

Being married to a sensible person is a great defense. One of you may be fooled, but it's harder to fool two people at the same time. If your spouse has doubts when you are asked to trust someone other than the Lord, pay attention to his or her wariness, ask some tough questions, and be very sure the person in question is worthy of your trust.

Father, we know You are the only one who deserves our complete confidence.
Give us the discernment we need and show us what we should do
when we are asked to follow someone else.

Being a neighbor entails a certain amount of responsibility. As humans, we live near others for sociability, mutual support, and safety. If there weren't benefits to dwelling in neighborhoods, we'd all be living as far apart as possible, an appealing thought when the teenager upstairs turns up the volume and rattles your teeth.

> Do not devise evil against your neighbor, for he dwells by you for safety's sake.
> PROVERBS 3:29 NKJV

When a couple moves into a new neighborhood, they have to adjust to those already in place. Some neighborhoods are close communities, while others are just a collection of unrelated individuals who want to be left alone.

But as long as mutual respect exists in the neighborhood, you can live near almost anyone.

Father, help us be good neighbors wherever we live,
willing to help others whenever possible.

> Therefore glorify the LORD
> in the dawning light.
> ISAIAH 24:15 NKJV

It's hard to glorify God while concentrating on shaving or trying to get everyone up and out on time. No one has time for more than the bare essentials at dawn, but the beginning of a new day is a precious gift that should be welcomed and for which we should give thanks. How can a couple find time for this when they can't even sit down and eat breakfast together?

We tend to think of worship as an institutional event, but it doesn't always have to be so. You can pray for your children as you pack their lunches or sing a doxology in the shower. Opening the blinds and feeling the sun cross your face can be a religious experience, as can watching your children climb onto the school bus, filled with expectations of a good day.

You don't always need a congregation to worship; it's enough that God hears your thanksgiving for this day.

Father, we do appreciate the blessing of each new day.
Make Yourself such a constant presence in our lives that we are able to
worship You at any place, in any situation.

Are you and your spouse at about the same place spiritually, or is one further along the figurative road of faith? To be at different points in the journey is not unusual, nor is it an invitation to problems as long as mutual respect is alive and well in the relationship. Problems may, however, arise if one of you decides you are "superior" to the other or attempts to "lead" the other.

> And let us consider how we may spur one another on toward love and good deeds.
> HEBREWS 10:24 NIV

Neither of those two words appears in the Scripture verse above. Note especially that "spurring" someone involves encouragement, and not sharp, pointed objects. If you are ever tempted to preach to your partner or belittle his or her faith, examine your motives honestly. Is something other than faith the issue here? Are you using religion as a weapon and not a blessing? Do you have the love and patience necessary to show Jesus' love through example and trust the rest to Him?

*Father, it's much harder to serve as a good example
than it is to demand faith from another.
Give us both patience as we grow in our faith together.*

The Old Testament is filled with harsh stories that contain violence and sacrifice, things we would rather not think about, let alone deal with in our own lives. Such a view, though, obscures the richness and wisdom that may be found in each and every ancient text of God's Word. This weekend why not spend some time in what was Jesus' Bible, and discover for yourselves some priceless "nuggets" that will enrich your modern-day lives.

Find one individual in the Old Testament with whom you can identify and then trace his or her life. Woven among the stories are every human emotion: heroism and foolishness, love and hatred, denial and acceptance. For action and suspense, the Bible easily surpasses any of today's bestsellers.

No one expects us to be cheerful and happy in the face of bad times. We may be Christians, but we bleed and cry just as much as nonbelievers.

> When times are good, be happy;
> but when times are bad, consider:
> God has made the one
> as well as the other.
> ECCLESIASTES 7:14 NIV

You probably know at least one couple that has gone through terrible suffering with tremendous faith and fortitude. How do they cope? What do they know that you don't? More than likely, they have taken to heart the second part of the above verse: "When times are bad, consider: God has made the one as well as the other." Good and bad, happy and sad, everything comes from God. We may not like some of the things He gives us, but He has His own reasons beyond our understanding, and everything is part of His plan.

Father, it's hard to give thanks for pain.
Grant us the wisdom to accept Your plan for our lives,
even when it hurts, for we know everything comes from You.

_____ TUESDAY _____

> "Restrain your voice from weeping and your eyes from tears, for your work will be rewarded," declares the LORD.
>
> JEREMIAH 31:16 NIV

Are you tempted to sigh, "But not in this life," when you read this verse? That's one of the difficult parts of being human: You don't always get the reward you deserve at what you consider the appropriate time, which is while you're alive to enjoy it!

Still, you have hope. Maybe you're only one promotion away from your reward. Maybe when you retire you will garner all the rewards you deserve. Maybe when you have grandchildren or great-grandchildren you'll at last have what you've been missing. Or maybe in the next life, in heaven. . . .

Waiting until we get to heaven is asking for a lot of patience. Still, the promise is there: "Your work *will be* rewarded." Believe the promise, and you really have no need for weeping or tears. What do you have to lose?

Lord, we do believe that all Your promises will be kept.
Forgive us our impatience and lack of faith,
and help us lean on You when we are discouraged.

You might say David was having a very bad day. He was sure God had forsaken him, and his enemies pressed even closer, more than happy to take advantage of his weakened position. We all have days like that, as individuals and couples. David, however, remembered what most of us forget at times like this: God had already forgiven him.

> You know my reproach,
> my shame, and my dishonor;. . .
> Reproach has broken my heart,
> and I am full of heaviness;
> I looked for someone to take pity,
> but there was none;
> and for comforters, but I found none.
> PSALM 69:19–20 NKJV

If you can't find an earthly friend willing to comfort you or have pity on you when you need it, look to the One who knows you the best. Ask His forgiveness and get on with your life, secure in the knowledge of God's love.

Father, there are times when no one can make us feel better,
when they laugh at our faith and try to take advantage of us.
But we know Your love is never ending,
Your compassion without bounds.

> Whoever robs his father
> or his mother, and says,
> "It is no transgression,"
> the same is companion to
> a destroyer.
> PROVERBS 28:24 NKJV

For some reason, we tend to think that we can sin against our family without guilt, doing things to them we would not think of doing to a stranger. Maybe it's because they have always forgiven us our faults (something parents do well!). But when we continually treat our family unfairly, we eat away at the mutual respect and love that exists among family members and may end up losing our strongest, most supportive friends.

Do you "rob" your parents without thinking twice? Do you put off visiting them, preferring to spend your free time in another way? Do you borrow from them with no intention of repaying? Does your busyness keep them from having a real relationship with their grandchildren? How long can a parent be expected to give and give, receiving nothing in return?

Father, our parents are a constant source of support to us, asking little in return.
Help us find ways to repay them, whether it be in time or attention,
because they need us as much as we need them.

_____

_____

_____

_____

_____

_____

_____

_____

_____

_____

We begin to see some things a little more clearly as we age. Maybe that's because we see fewer of the details and have enough experience to know when we can safely and fairly generalize. What David saw as he grew older was that the righteous received the help they needed from God, and even their children were blessed. Certainly there were times when the righteous suffered, but in the long run they prospered.

> I have been young, and now am old; yet have I not seen the righteous forsaken, nor his seed begging bread.
> PSALM 37:25 KJV

Perusing the daily newspaper, you realize "good" people don't make for good news. Righteousness is a bore. Look around your own neighborhood, church, and family. Aren't there more "good" people than bad? And, in the long run, haven't the good been blessed? Don't let someone else tell you how terrible the world is and how the good are always punished. Look for yourself; use your own eyes.

Lord, give us eyes to see the whole truth,
not just what someone else decides is the truth.
You still uphold those who love You.

_____SATURDAY_____

> "Son of man,
> with one blow I am about to take away
> from you the delight of your eyes.
> Yet do not lament or weep or shed any tears.
> Groan quietly; do not mourn for the dead. . . ."
> So I spoke to the people in the morning,
> and in the evening my wife died.
> The next morning I did
> as I had been commanded.
> EZEKIEL 24:16–18 NIV

Can you imagine the strength Ezekiel must have had to obey God? The Old Testament prophet loved his wife deeply, and you can almost hear the compassion in God's words as He warns His servant that this blow is going to hurt. Why did God do such a thing to someone so faithful?

The reason soon becomes obvious. Ezekiel was to be a living example for the Israelites, who were about to see Jerusalem destroyed. They were to be as strong as Ezekiel in their grief, and they would need a living, breathing, hurting person to be their model.

"I did as I had been commanded," Ezekiel says. By the terseness of his words we can tell that he was not happy about his sacrifice. Yet he did as he had been commanded for the glory of God and the good of his people. Anytime you think God is asking too much of you, put yourself in Ezekiel's sandals.

Lord, just the thought of losing my mate scares me to death,
let alone not being able to mourn such a loss.
The next time I feel put upon by Your wishes,
remind me of Ezekiel's strength and sacrifice.

Think back on the times you thought God was overloading you with demands you could not possibly obey. What kind of sacrifice was required? Were you able to do God's will, or do you think you failed? As you look back, do you find you did better than you thought at the time, or worse?

And thine ears shall hear
a word behind thee, saying,
This is the way, walk ye in it,
when ye turn to the right hand,
and when ye turn to the left.
ISAIAH 30:21 KJV

Notice that this verse doesn't say you'll never wander off the right path. Our desire to go smell the flowers elsewhere can be overwhelming, as can our sheer stubbornness. "It's only a little detour," one might say. "I can get back on the right path anytime I want. I know exactly where it is."

If you've ever done any wilderness hiking, you know how dangerous wandering off the path can be, and how easily you can get turned around and lost. Right now you and your spouse are hiking through life together. That's good, because hiking alone can be scary, not to mention dangerous. You need to listen when your spouse has misgivings about a turn you want to take. You need to consult each other, read the map God has provided, and not allow yourselves to be tempted off the path and into the wilderness.

Father, whenever one of us hears Your warning voice,
make the other take the alarm seriously.
Help us not to continue on the wrong path,
trusting more in ourselves than in You.

_____

_____

_____

_____

_____

_____

_____

_____

_____

_____

_____

_____

_____

_____

Some people seem to enjoy seeing a Christian fall flat on his face. After all, the "world" expects us to be perfect and there are those who feel a little smug when we aren't. The sad part is, some of those sneering at us are fellow Christians who should know better.

> Rejoice not against me,
> O mine enemy:
> when I fall, I shall arise;
> when I sit in darkness,
> the Lord shall be a light unto me.
> MICAH 7:8 KJV

There will be days when you, as a couple, will feel others looking at you with disappointment. Perhaps you are having problems in your marriage, or one of your children is going through a rebellious stage, or you have sinned and been found out. You may have tripped but you can always get up again. Keep your eyes on the Lord, your head high, and walk on.

Lord, we all stumble and fall.
When we do, and others see our problems,
let us be good witnesses for You by confessing our sins and walking on,
secure in Your forgiveness.

"I have labored to no purpose;
I have spent my strength in vain
and for nothing.
Yet what is due me is in the LORD's hand,
and my reward is with my God."
ISAIAH 49:4 NIV

We've all had disastrous days. Maybe a special project went down in flames after weeks of work, or you totaled an almost-new car, or, much worse, a child took the wrong path. All that time gone to waste, all that effort for nothing! It's enough to make you look for another job, start riding a bike, or throw your hands up in frustration.

Deep in your heart, though, you know you are not a failure. You did the best you could but circumstances defeated you this time. The next time you could very well win. The Lord knows how hard you worked and, no matter what the outcome, the Lord will reward you for your effort.

Lord, be with us when we face failure in our lives.
Be our strength and give us the will to press on,
knowing our reward is in Your hands.

Working parents and stay-at-home moms and dads
agree: We don't have enough time with our children. It's only natural that when we are with
them, we want those hours to be filled with fun,
and not lectures. Yet it is the duty of parents to be
teachers and not best buddies, and we are not doing
right by our children unless we teach them how to live in a
godly manner.

> "Teach them the decrees and laws,
> and show them the way to live and
> the duties they are to perform."
> EXODUS 18:20 NIV

Who else is going to teach them manners? Who else cares as much about their honesty and decency?

Instead of lectures, though, we should strive to give them constant, positive examples.
Through your own lives you will teach them what you value. If you want Christian children, you must live as Christian parents.

Father, bringing up our children is our job, and not one for society.
When we are being bad examples, show us our errors.
Be our teacher so we may teach our children how to live in faith.

_____FRIDAY_____

> "Who of you by worrying
> can add a single hour
> to his life?"
>
> MATTHEW 6:27 NIV

We have an awful lot to worry about today, especially if we are parents. In a short time the world can turn us into bitter, disappointed people who see no hope for the future. But worrying about life isn't the answer.

Worrying about money doesn't make you more money. Worrying about love doesn't make you lovable, either. Worry brings you absolutely nothing good. The next time you catch yourself sitting at the kitchen table worrying about something you can't control, bake cookies or go mow the lawn. Doing something useful will set your worries free.

Father, our lives are in Your hands, and we know You love us.
Turn our worries into constructive behavior that will bring glory to You and peace to us.

In biblical times hospitality was expected of everyone, even at times meaning the difference between life and death if the next source of food and water was miles away. But while hospitality may no longer be so critical physically, it can be a spiritual life-and-death matter for the nongiver. Today no one has time to entertain. We collapse in front of the TV, thankful for a little peace and quiet. We don't even know our neighbors. We become more and more isolated, more dependent on ourselves, and more cut off from everyone else.

Use hospitality one to another without grudging.
1 PETER 4:9 KJV

A Christian couple needs fellowship with others. They need to see how other Christians are managing their lives. They need the input of older couples whom they can emulate. They need to be part of something bigger than themselves, and they need the love and support of other believers.

Father, help us make time for others in our lives
so they can aid our growth as Christians
through the fellowship we all require.

It's the time of year for April Fool's Day. One sign of real intimacy is the ability to be silly with someone without having to worry about what that person thinks. Do you know that your spouse accepts you when you're silly, and even enjoys it?

If you have trouble being silly together, why do you feel that way? What can you do about it?

Spend time together doing something silly or relaxing. *Fun* is the word for today. Enjoy!

"Marriage takes a lot of work," you'll hear people say, until you wonder if they're planning a forty-hour work week for marriage, on top of your career.

> May your fountain be blessed, and may you rejoice in the wife of your youth.
>
> PROVERBS 5:18 NIV

If by "work" they mean you have to treat each other well, settle differences, and stick together through the hard times, perhaps they're right. But if they mean that marriage is just drudgery, nothing could be further from God's truth.

God didn't make marriage to be painful. He wants to give two people an opportunity to serve Him, enjoy each other, and share happiness and troubles. When we put Him first in our marriages and follow His rules for love, we rejoice in our spouses. Even when we face trouble, God's grace lifts us up and enables us to take delight in our mates.

Are you rejoicing today?

Lord, we don't want our marriage to be drudgery.
If we aren't rejoicing, show us where we need to draw closer to You
so we can come nearer to each other.

_____ TUESDAY _____

> He that blesseth his friend
> with a loud voice,
> rising early in the morning,
> it shall be counted a curse to him.
> PROVERBS 27:14 KJV

It's true for friends *and* spouses. Wake up someone who's not a morning person with loud praises and he'll resent it. All he wants at 5 A.M. is his bed.

Chances are one of you wakes up early, ready to go, while the other wants time to unwrap sleep from his or her body. Maybe the same person who wakes up early is snoozing in a chair by 10 P.M.

God made our engines run at different speeds and get started at different times. You can make that work to your advantage by getting up early and starting the coffee while your spouse snoozes, or by taking the wheel for your mate during that nighttime drive, when she's sacked out in the passenger's seat.

Just don't fight that body-clock thing: It's a losing battle.

Lord, You sure made us different, even if we are married.
Help us to use those differences for our benefit instead of fighting them.

Could people look at your marriage and convict you of being a Christian? Or would they see nothing different about your relationship? Your marriage testifies to the new life faith in God brings. Your marriage is a physical sign of whatever is in your hearts.

> Get rid of all bitterness, rage and anger, brawling and slander, along with every form of malice.
>
> EPHESIANS 4:31 NIV

Friends, family, and even bystanders will notice if you constantly snipe at each other with bitter remarks, scream at the top of your voices, and try to make each other look bad by obvious or deceptive means. They won't see anything different from the world's values, and they won't believe in your God.

Paul encouraged the Ephesians to live differently from others by ridding themselves of negative emotions that destroyed their Christian testimony and, through Christ, by putting on the positive emotions that would let people see Jesus in their lives. We need to do that, too.

Lord Jesus, convict others of their need for faith through our marriage. Make us a bright light, shining Your love for all to see.

When one mate holds a grudge against the other, the signs of conflict radiate from both partners.

> Be kind and compassionate to one another, forgiving each other, just as in Christ God forgave you.
> EPHESIANS 4:32 NIV

A marriage without kindness, compassion, and forgiveness lacks the oil that makes a relationship run smoothly. Because grudges remain and are constantly pointed out, a load of "sand" has destroyed a fine-tuned machine. Suddenly its engine grinds to a halt. What you have isn't a relationship anymore—it's a wreck.

The damage probably began with sin. Undoubtedly, there was something the hurt partner "just couldn't" forgive. Instead of seeking resolution, the couple took the easy way out and traded hurtful barbs. Kindness and compassion went to the side, and emotional sniping took its place.

If your relationship has sand in it, wash it out with forgiveness and fill it with kindness and compassion. Don't turn your marriage into a broken-down engine but into a fine-tuned machine for God.

Lord, we don't want to battle each other instead of Satan.
Show us how to make forgiveness, kindness, and compassion flow in our marriage.

_____

_____

_____

_____

_____

_____

_____

_____

_____

_____

_____

Two people sharing a marriage have plenty of opportunity to see each other's flaws.

Sometimes we have to hold each other to account and suggest a change. To fail to do so would be to treat marriage irresponsibly. Not surprisingly, a mate may not respond well to that information.

> "Or how can you say to your brother,
> 'Let me remove the speck from your eye';
> and look, a plank is in your own eye?. . .
> First remove the plank from your own eye."
> MATTHEW 7:4–5 NKJV

So, before you point out anything, ask yourself if you've contributed to the situation. If you have, start by asking forgiveness from God and your mate. Then be aware of the sensitive places in your spouse's heart. Forgiveness, not harsh criticism, needs to cushion your discussion.

Finally, change doesn't come easily to any of us, and it may take time. A correcting partner also needs to be a patient partner.

Thank You, God, that, through You,
we can make changes in our lives.
Help us to be sensitive to each other,
when we need to correct or be corrected.

> The LORD will give
> strength to His people;
> the LORD will bless
> His people with peace.
> PSALM 29:11 NKJV

Trying to live with another person can be frustrating. There may be family troubles, a rebellious or ill child, or a lost job. Sometimes frustration comes from disappointment with your mate. But all your skies don't have to be blue before you start enjoying a peaceful marriage.

Despite what the world tells you, peace doesn't start with you or your spouse. If you relied only on each other, you'd always fail. People always *do* fail, one way or the other.

As Christians, your peace comes from God. Recognize that daily and you'll see a great change in your emotions for each other. Start praising God together and living for Him, despite your troubles, and your marriage can't help but improve.

No matter the circumstances you find yourself in today, God can give your marriage strength and peace. He may not solve every problem overnight, but He'll enable you to overcome each one.

Praise You, Lord God, for Your strength and the peace we have through knowing You.
Work through our lives to do Your will.

_____

_____

_____

_____

_____

_____

_____

_____

_____

_____

_____

_____

_____

_____

Is your marriage a blessing?

If your answer is less than enthusiastic, what has contributed to that off-the-cuff feeling? Do you each have irritating habits that you have not tried to curb? Do you use them against each other? Have negative emotions built up in your hearts? Or have a good prayer life, active communication, and shared experiences brought you a blessed marriage?

Discuss the rough spots and blessings in your marriage. Can you see things that have contributed to them? Do you need to make some improvements?

This weekend, if possible, return to a place where you remember feeling truly blessed. This could be the campus where you met or a beautiful park you visited when you were engaged. Maybe it's a spot where you felt a great blessing from God.

But whatever you do, spend time thanking God for your marriage and praising Him for His greatness.

> If we let him thus alone,
> all men will believe on him:
> and the Romans shall come and
> take away both our place and nation.
> JOHN 11:48 KJV

Jesus had just raised Lazarus from the dead. But instead of rejoicing, the Pharisees called a "what do we do now to protect our turf?" meeting. Afraid they would lose their authority, they wanted to control the situation.

Marriage has its power plays, too. Instead of looking out for the good of our relationship, one of us decides to win at any cost. *My way is right*, that spouse thinks. *It's only fair I should make this decision.* That person plans to win and turns a marriage into a soul-rending struggle.

Power plays didn't solve the Pharisees' problems, and they won't solve yours, either. Badly used, power destroys a nation—or a family.

Lord, we want to serve You, not fight each other for power.
Keep our hearts on You, not our "authority."

There was something funny about the way this "spiritual" treasurer always looked to the bottom line. Odd that a pure man like Jesus was served by one so dishonest! Judas didn't really care about the poor; he wanted to place that money in his own pocket.

> Why was not this ointment sold for three hundred pence, and given to the poor? This he said. . . because he was a thief.
> JOHN 12:5–6 KJV

Why did Jesus, who surely knew what was in His disciple's heart, trust Judas with that money? we wonder.

Two thousand years later, things haven't changed much. Jesus still gives dishonest disciples money. Some lease a new car when they could buy an old one for His service. Others buy unnecessary Christmas gifts, while across town people starve during the holidays.

Jesus gives us money to spend for Him every day, as if we were the most honest of His followers. He trusts us, even if we've wasted it before. When we fail, He only asks that we turn to Him for forgiveness.

Even Judas might have done that.

*We're humbled, Lord, to think how much You trust us, despite our sins.
Turn us to You for forgiveness, each time we fail.*

> Believe me that
> I am in the Father,
> and the Father *in* me:
> or else believe me
> for the very works' sake.
> JOHN 14:11 KJV

I would have loved to walk with Jesus, each of us thinks at some time, imagining that seeing Jesus would have made a faith walk easier. But living day to day with Him for three years, twelve ordinary men often felt confused by their Master, Jesus. Friendship with Him included sudden miracles, cryptic sayings, and prophecies of a dark future. No wonder Philip had a confused picture of the relationship between the Master and the Father!

Sometimes our picture of God becomes equally fuzzy. We obey God in a tough situation—and things just get worse. We think we have a clear picture of Him, only to find we have much more to learn. Living with Jesus in our hearts isn't always a piece of cake.

A Christian's journey with Jesus—whether walking in His earthly footsteps or following the steps shown us in His Word—is a walk of faith. It's a journey in which seeing isn't believing, but believing *is* seeing.

We don't always find it easy to trust You, Lord.
Stir our hearts to faith even when our minds become confused.

The high priest wasn't really interested in what Jesus taught or the people who followed Him. He was searching for a loophole. The goal was to be able legally to get rid of this man who threatened Israel's religious machine.

> The high priest then asked Jesus of his disciples, and of his doctrine.
>
> JOHN 18:19 KJV

We've run into similar situations. A friend starts asking questions about our faith, but we quickly figure that she isn't really interested in what we believe. She's looking for an argument. Her goal is to "legally" prove that Christianity doesn't work.

Words are unlikely to change such friends. Chances are slim that even a perfect argument will prove God's "case." Arguments about the Christian faith usually aren't made by minds that want convincing but by empty hearts. Arguers need to know, deep down inside, that there is a God who loves them unconditionally.

Words may partially convince them of that truth, but the loving actions in our marriage may bring it to life.

Lord Jesus, by giving up Your life,
You clearly showed what no discussion could prove.
We want our lives to show Your truth, too.

_____FRIDAY_____

> It is finished:
> and he bowed his head,
> and gave up the ghost.
> JOHN 19:30 KJV

It was all over: the illegal trial, the brutal punishment, the crying of the disciples beneath the cross. The hearts of Jesus' followers were broken as they saw every hope and dream wiped out by the wicked religious leaders of Jerusalem. How could the men in authority have missed God's point? Even faith itself seemed finished.

Like the disciples, we've faced places where outwardly faith failed to triumph. But even when bright prospects seem tarnished, if we give up hope, we've forgotten God's promises. He had told those first-century followers of His Resurrection, but their clouded minds couldn't imagine it. Neither can we envision all the glories of His Second Coming.

Even when it seems finished, life isn't over until God has His last word—and when that word is new life, it isn't over at all!

Our hopes, Lord Jesus, rely on You,
not our earthly circumstances.
Our praises belong to You, even on the darkest days.

_____

_____

_____

_____

_____

_____

_____

_____

_____

_____

For three years John had followed Jesus. Then, in one divine moment, the truth connected, and suddenly the disciple knew that this was Messiah, the one for whom his heart had searched.

> Then went in also that other disciple, which came first to the sepulchre, and he saw, and believed.
> JOHN 20:8 KJV

Meeting the right man or woman and "just clicking" can seem delightful. You've never experienced such intimacy, and you marry. But even a satisfying marriage pales beside knowing Jesus truly and deeply.

Through Him we understand ourselves and each other more clearly. Jesus cleans out the dirty spaces in our hearts and gives us true joy. He can make marriage wonderful, but no marriage—even one provided and blessed by Him—can fill the places He fills in our hearts.

Nothing on this earth is truly divine, no matter how much we enjoy it. Nothing, not even a much-loved spouse, can take the place of God in our hearts.

Give Jesus first place in your heart, and award your spouse a close second. Then you both will win.

Thank You, Lord, for blessing us with this marriage.
But remind us daily that we are not "number one," You are.

Week 15

For most people Easter doesn't conjure up the childlike appeal of Christmas. The somber truths about sin's cost may overshadow the reality of God's grace. But the freedom from sin offered by salvation should make this a day for rejoicing.

Create an Easter time of joy and testimony in your family. (Do it with your immediate family, or even just between yourselves, if sharing with your larger family is not possible.) Share about the moment you believed, knowing that Jesus was God's Son who died for your sin, or outline the slow changes that brought you to recognize Him. Tell how you've given God first place in your life. Describe the joy Jesus has brought into your life. Celebrate all He has done for you.

_____

_____

_____

_____

_____

_____

_____

_____

_____

_____

_____

_____

_____

How many of us have been pierced through with sorrows over credit cards, mortgages, or plain, hard cash? Especially in marriage, where two people have to use money together, hitting a balance on money can be difficult.

> For the love of money is the root of all evil: which while some coveted after, they have erred from the faith, and pierced themselves through with many sorrows.
> 1 TIMOTHY 6:10 KJV

It's not so much a matter of how much money you have. Even if you have millions of dollars, you can still end up a pauper. Use a little frugally, and you may outdo that once-wealthy person. Money comes and goes during our lives.

God wants our love to be for Him, and not for money. Love, as created by God, isn't designed to be given to inanimate objects.

Has money taken a place before God, your spouse, and family? If so, your faith will be weak, your marriage troubled, and your relationships empty. No matter your bank account, you'll be poor.

Are you investing in people today or only your financial future?

Lord, keep our books balanced, but even more, keep our relationship healthy with love.

_____TUESDAY_____

> And Peter answered unto her,
> Tell me whether
> ye sold the land for so much?
> And she said, Yea, for so much. . . .
> Peter said. . . How is it that ye have agreed
> together to tempt the Spirit of the Lord?
> ACTS 5:8–9 KJV

Ananias and Sapphira may not have agreed on much in their marriage. Maybe they constantly argued over the household expenses, or maybe they had different goals for their income. But when it came to lying to the apostles about the price they got for land they sold, the two spoke as a single voice. Even when Peter caught them in a lie, neither admitted the sin or asked forgiveness. The spiritual death that gripped them cost the two their lives.

Some husbands and wives seem to find agreement on the wrong things; the partners think lying, infidelity, and other sins are fine—as long as they don't get caught. Those attitudes don't kill the couple off as rapidly as Ananias and Sapphira's did, but they are signs of spiritual death.

Christian marriages need to find agreement on many positive things: truths we recognize, family goals, and ways in which we can honor God. Are you in agreement today to honor God?

Lord, give us good agreement in our marriage.

_____ WEDNESDAY _____

_____

_____

_____

_____

_____

_____

_____

_____

_____

_____

_____

_____

Put two people together as husband and wife and either teamwork or a pulling contest results.

> Submitting yourselves one to another in the fear of God.
> EPHESIANS 5:21 KJV

Teamwork isn't a matter of one partner driving the other but of two pulling in the direction God has set for them. As they move in the same direction, in service to Him, they take each other into consideration. And that marriage grows.

Working as a team isn't always easy. Sometimes one team member becomes a "hot dog," trying to take all the glory; then the other member feels unimportant, and trouble ensues. At other times both members of the team go off in their own directions. Neither is productive.

But a smoothly working team that submits to the needs of each other is wonderful to watch. It has a set goal and the partners work in rhythm to accomplish it. When they seek to obey God, His will is done, and He is glorified.

In what direction is your marriage going?

A pulling contest isn't what we want our marriage to be, Lord.
Today head us in the direction You have for our shared lives.

_____THURSDAY_____

> Now. . .in the latter times
> some shall depart from the faith,
> giving heed to. . .doctrines of devils. . .
> forbidding to marry,
> and commanding to abstain from meats,
> which God hath created to be received
> with thanksgiving of them which
> believe and know the truth.
> 1 TIMOTHY 4:1, 3 KJV

God didn't set a trap in marriage. People who tell you you're foolish to be married don't know what they're talking about.

Paul describes people who would deny others the joy of marriage as being seduced by doctrines of devils. Deluded by Satan's call to immorality, these naysayers may think marriage just keeps you from "playing the field." Or perhaps they had bad family experiences. Surely they have not known the joy that God prepares for people who know Him and commit their lives together in Him.

Being married isn't any more wrong than eating meat is, says Paul.

Just as we need to thank God for our daily meals, we need to thank Him for our marriages. Enjoying the companionship of another person is a blessing from God, not a weakness.

Thank You, Father God, for Your many blessings in our lives.
We especially thank You for each other and the love we share.

_____

_____

_____

_____

_____

_____

_____

_____

_____

_____

_____

_____

_____

The way people handle money shows God a lot about their trustworthiness. God knows how much He can trust us with spiritual blessings when He looks at the way we handle our cash.

> If therefore ye have not been faithful in the unrighteous mammon, who will commit to your trust the true riches?
> LUKE 16:11 KJV

Have we blown our money on a new, expensive car when we couldn't pay our credit card bills? Then how can He trust us with spiritual authority over others? Won't we settle for the "convenient" thing there, too?

Though money has no heavenly value, financial decisions do have a spiritual impact. If yours is an "easy come, easy go" attitude, and your spouse can't trust you with the rent, God won't seriously expect to receive the tithe you promised Him in one short-lived, fervent burst of faith.

Do your spouse and God know you can be trusted with finances? That confidence is more priceless than any currency you could store in a bank.

Lord Jesus, we want to heed Your warning and show our love for You through our finances. May we be wise stewards of the money You have given us.

SATURDAY

A threefold cord is not quickly broken.

ECCLESIASTES 4:12 KJV

Working things out on your own can get tiring. Without the advice and strength of another, making decisions and directing your life can become wearying. When your spouse comes alongside to help, it can be a great blessing.

But even when together you head in the same direction and serve God with all your hearts, you can come to a roadblock. Neither of you can see the future. Should you spend money on redoing the house, because you'll eventually sell it for more, or should you bank that money for another need?

That's why it's important to have a third cord in your strand of decision making: God. Alone, you can make a devastating wrong choice. But when the Lord of time and space is at the center of your choices, even those that seem less than perfect will turn out fine.

One alone works hard and two are better. But the perfect solution is two relying on the One.

Thank You, Lord, that You care about our choices and want to help us make good ones.
Be the center of every decision we make.

One of the most frequently cited causes of divorce is money. Faced with a limited commodity, couples have to communicate well about their needs and future plans.

This weekend take a look at your finances together. If one of you usually takes care of the bills, bring the other up to date on your situation. If your checkbook needs balancing, catch up on that. Take a look at the investments you have for the future or talk about those you'd like to establish and how you can do it.

What dreams do you have that will take some money? Talk about the things you'd like to do and when you'd like to do them. If necessary, start planning for your future.

_____MONDAY_____

> Let not my lord. . .regard. . .
> Nabal: for as his name is, so is he;
> Nabal is his name,
> and folly is with him.
> 1 SAMUEL 25:25 KJV

Imagine being married to a man whose name meant "foolish." Abigail was, but worse than that, her husband, Nabal, lived up to his name. Though David had protected Nabal's sheep, Abigail's imprudent spouse spoke rudely to his defender. The message this wealthy man sent put his household in danger, as David decided to kill every man in it.

God blessed Nabal with a wife who averted the disaster by her wise words. But obviously Abigail didn't appreciate the chore.

Abigail isn't the only one who doesn't like to clean up a spouse's mouth mess. If your spouse often bails you out of the consequences of your unwise words, life won't be peaceful. Like Abigail, your mate may be quick to admit your faults to others, and you'll soon have a well-earned reputation.

Seeking wisdom from God and treating others well, including your spouse, won't earn you the nickname "Foolish." Is it a name you'd like to try on for size?

Probably not.

Give us wisdom, Lord, in our dealings with people, especially with each other.

_____

_____

_____

_____

_____

_____

_____

_____

_____

_____

_____

You never read about Priscilla without Aquila mentioned alongside, and vice versa. In Scripture, this couple's successes are always shared.

> So he [Apollos] began to speak boldly in the synagogue. When Aquila and Priscilla heard him, they took him aside and explained to him the way of God more accurately.
> ACTS 18:26 NKJV

Apollos didn't have the whole story on the Bible, a situation Priscilla and Aquila decided to remedy. But Aquila didn't say, "Dear, you go home while I counsel with Apollos." And Priscilla didn't claim, "I have more Bible knowledge than you do, darling, so I'm the best one for the job." They worked together to bring a man who was already "mighty in the Scriptures" (v. 24, NKJV) to a more complete understanding.

Marriage isn't designed to be a spiritual competition. Scripture doesn't tell us Priscilla was fighting to have more Bible studies or followers than Aquila, or that Aquila was trying to get more kudos from Paul. They worked as a team, one always linked in Scripture.

Teamwork allows two people to reach the world for Christ!

Lord God, we don't want to argue about rights, we want to serve You.
Turn us into Your powerful team.

> Greet Priscilla and Aquila,
> my fellow workers in Christ Jesus,
> who risked their own necks for my life,
> to whom not only I give thanks,
> but also all the churches
> of the Gentiles.
> ROMANS 16:3–4 NKJV

Priscilla and Aquila are mentioned only a few times in the Bible. While they don't have the commanding place of apostles, without them the Gospel might never have come to the Gentiles through Paul.

Jewish Aquila and his wife somehow risked their safety for the life of the apostle to the Gentiles. Without them a worldwide church formed by Paul's ministry might never have existed. After all, people didn't exactly stand in line to endanger their lives for the apostle.

Through an act of obedience, one first-century couple affected millions who never met them—an entire Gentile world, covering numerous nations.

Every person who knows God is designed to reach out to many. One act by two Christians can even influence a whole world.

Are you touching Planet Earth today?

*Though we may never preach to multitudes,
we want to influence others for You, Lord. Show us how.*

God gifts each of His people with spiritual abilities that serve the church and the world. Some are wonderful preachers, others provide strong testimonies, while still others offer comfort to hurting spirits.

> There are diversities of gifts, but the same Spirit. There are differences of ministries, but the same Lord.
> 1 CORINTHIANS 12:4–5 NKJV

This diversity of gifts could hardly be contained in one person. Who would have time to do every good work or be in every place at the same time? That's why God gave gifts to each Christian.

Every marriage contains a collection of spiritual gifts. A wife may be a great comforter, while her husband easily reaches out to those in pain. Or a great preacher may marry a great organizer who helps keep their life in order.

Those gifts aren't meant to start competition in a marriage, but to benefit others, including your mate. Both of you serve the same Lord, even if your gifts differ. You can use them to reach the world for Christ—or waste time arguing over which set of gifts is "better."

Lord, thank You for giving us gifts that are "best" in Your sight.
Help us to serve You faithfully with them.

> "Therefore everyone who hears these words of mine and puts them into practice is like a wise man who built his house on the rock."
>
> MATTHEW 7:24 NIV

You've probably seen wristbands with the abbreviation "WWJD," or "What would Jesus do?" But have you seen the T-shirt asking, "What would Martha do?"

Even people who don't think they follow anybody will decorate their houses in a certain style or make food in a certain fashion. That's fine—after all, we shouldn't have to reinvent the wheel every day for ordinary things. But we don't need to follow a decorator's every utterance. She doesn't have that kind of authority.

Just as we look for advice on home-decorating styles, we often follow people with spiritual "styles." It may be a church leader who has a warm personality that draws others to him, a friend who has good values, or someone in the office whom we admire. But unless that person emulates Jesus, by following him or her we may be nicely decorating a house built on sand, instead of making sure we're the contractor for a house built on the Rock.

Lord, don't let us waste our time "decorating" a weak spiritual house that needs to be made strong by You.

Before you were born God knew just what you would be like. Light skin or dark? Fair, straight hair or glossy dark ringlets? Easily tempted to become angry, or one who goes with the flow?

> O LORD, you have searched me
> and you know me. . . .
> You are familiar with all my ways.
> PSALM 139:1, 3 NIV

You and your spouse grew up in homes with diverse family backgrounds. You came out of your environments as different people. Maybe one went to college while the other went straight to work.

You started dating and found common ground, but once you married, those differences cropped up again. *Can two such opposite people share the same marriage?* you might wonder.

Take heart. God didn't mean you to be duplicates.

Marital contrasts can strengthen that relationship if a couple shares them instead of treating each other's ideas as alien territory. Handled well, differing attitudes and abilities create a deeper relationship, not a battleground.

Don't fight over differences. Rather, deal lovingly and intelligently with them, and you'll develop a stronger marriage, fusing your strengths and limiting your weaknesses.

God knew you weren't identical—even twins aren't exactly the same!

Lord, help us understand our differences and use them to strengthen our marriage.

She likes to fish, while he hates getting his hands wet. He'll spend all day shopping for two tools, while she has a long list, goes to the mall, picks up her items, and runs for home in a couple of hours.

No two people do everything the same; it's one of the things that makes living in the same marriage a challenge. (But don't think that living with a friend would be any easier. We *all* have different ways of doing things!)

Sit down and discuss a few things you like to do that your spouse doesn't enjoy or ways that you do the same thing differently. Then try sharing your spouse's perspective while you do that thing together. Talk about why you enjoy—or don't enjoy—that chore or pastime.

You may not want to go shopping for tools with your spouse next time, but at least you'll understand why he takes so long!

_____

_____

_____

_____

_____

_____

_____

_____

_____

_____

_____

_____

_____

"You can't get something for nothing" might be a variation on this verse. Dine with a seemingly generous evil man, and you may find yourself trapped in his web of deceit. You can't play with evil and not get caught. Sooner or later the real person, the one in the evil man's heart, will come out.

> Eat thou not the bread of him that hath an evil eye,
> neither desire thou his dainty meats:
> For as he thinketh in his heart, so is he.
> PROVERBS 23:6–7 KJV

Maybe you've gotten a tempting job offer, but the company isn't quite honest. You've heard the local scuttlebutt or read about the company's questionable practices in the papers.

Before you say yes to that job, check it out. Take time to pray. Think about the cost of risking your reputation, even for a generous salary.

You may eat well for a while, but you don't want your heart tainted. Or even if you don't follow in your boss's footsteps, that negative reputation may follow you for years.

When we get a tempting offer, Lord, help us to see into the hearts of those who make it. We want to serve You, not the evil one.

> Ye shall not steal,
> neither deal falsely,
> neither lie one to another.
> LEVITICUS 19:11 KJV

Trustworthiness is the key to a good marriage. Without it, even the most loving of couples will have problems. But like all things that must be earned, to develop trustworthiness takes time.

Trust is built up during courtship. While no one sensible would marry someone he or she knows can't be trusted, there is a special type of trust that belongs to marriage. As you mature together, the trust between you becomes deeper.

Along the way you learn to call when you will be late for dinner, how to make coffee exactly the way your spouse likes it, and how to hold the baby properly. Then, somewhere along the line, the trust between you becomes absolute. Your husband lets you drive his new car without going through a litany of "do nots." Your wife lets you take the children camping for the weekend without checking to see that you packed everything you could possibly need. Finally, it dawns on you one day that this person would actually sacrifice his or her own life to save yours—without hesitation or second thoughts—and you would do the same for him or her.

That's a little frightening! That's trust.

Father, help us build trust in each other as the years go by,
until we are totally comfortable with each other
and know we have nothing to fear from the one we love.

How do you as a couple handle your money? Do you own everything jointly, or do you each have your own checking and savings accounts? Do you have wills that reflect the realities of your lives and your responsibilities? Do you have enough insurance? Are you saving for your children's education and investing for your retirement?

> Let no man seek his own, but every man another's wealth.
> 1 CORINTHIANS 10:24 KJV

The details of how you handle your money are important, but not as important as your attitude toward them. It's vital that you both agree to whatever arrangement you work out. Some wives will feel perfectly comfortable putting everything into joint accounts and letting their husbands handle everything. Others will feel nervous with such an arrangement. It's important that you discuss these matters with honesty and consideration for each other and come to mutually acceptable decisions.

Father, we both bring our own financial history into marriage and will disagree on some details. Help us come to an agreement that is based on love and consideration for each other.

For ye shall go out with joy,
and be led forth with peace:
the mountains and the hills
shall break forth before you into singing,
and all the trees of the field
shall clap their hands.

ISAIAH 55:12 KJV

At first the idea of animated hills and trees may seem silly. But go back in your mind and recall the happiest moment of your life—your wedding day, the day your first child was born, or the day you accepted Jesus as your Lord. A day totally unlike any other. The sunlight was so bright, the air so clear! Can't you still feel the gentle touch of the breeze on your face, hear the songs of the birds, see the greenness of the grass and the dance of the trees? Your senses were more acute than ever before and the whole world sang with you.

This is an earthly experience of the joy of the Lord, a joy so total and so amazing that you just want to laugh out loud and run in circles until you collapse. And who's to say the hills can't sing or the trees can't clap their hands on such a day?

*Lord, You fill our lives with joy beyond our understanding,
and we thank You for these precious times.*

You knew your spouse wasn't perfect when you married, but you didn't know he snored like an elephant! That's not one of the questions we generally ask before offering or accepting an engagement ring. On the other hand, you forgot to mention that you cut your toenails in the living room. What's the big deal?

Who can discern his errors?
Forgive my hidden faults.
PSALM 19:12 NIV

Most of the things that drive us crazy in a marriage were never mentioned in advance. They are truly "hidden" faults, those things a person does without realizing they might bug another. Indeed, a snorer rarely hears his own snores and will vehemently deny that he snores at all. And if everyone in your family clipped their toenails in such a manner, you assumed it was perfectly normal behavior. Have patience with each other, change what can be changed, and laugh at the rest.

*Father, when our hidden faults suddenly appear in our marriage,
help us understand they are mostly harmless, unconscious habits.
Help us change what can be changed and accept what cannot be changed.*

> Yet I will rejoice in the LORD,
> I will joy in the God
> of my salvation.
> HABAKKUK 3:18 KJV

When you read the first word of the verse, you know it follows a lot of trouble. "Yet. . ." means "in spite of. . ." or "but. . ." or "still. . . ." Things have gone terribly wrong, "yet. . . ." In a way, "yet" is a comforting word because you know things are about to change for the better.

We use words the same way today. "Honey, I had a little accident, but everything's fine." It's that conjunction—that "but"—that lets the listener stop holding her breath and slows her heartbeat. That little word says that nothing is hopeless, no matter how bad the news.

The next time you are dealing with a disaster or something that scares you to death, get to the "yet" as soon as possible. Then you and your partner can deal with the problem together and reach the place where you can rejoice in the Lord, the God of your salvation.

Father, our problems sometimes seem overwhelming,
yet we know good times are still in our future if we lean on You.

Spring has finally decided to hang around for a while. It's time to get out of the gym, off the treadmill, and out the door. Why not try a new sport this weekend, something you can do together? Borrow some bikes and really see your neighborhood, try trail riding, make fools of yourselves on a tennis court, or take a hike in a park. You don't have to be good at whatever you choose to try, and it certainly should not involve serious competition between you. Just get out and have some healthy fun together. Experiences like these keep you close to each other and give you something to share throughout your life.

_____ MONDAY _____

> Live a life of love,
> just as Christ loved us
> and gave himself up for us
> as a fragrant offering
> and sacrifice to God.
> EPHESIANS 5:2 NIV

Sacrifice is required in a marriage. Instead of playing in the Saturday morning baseball game, you stay home and cut the grass. Instead of going out to dinner on payday with the rest of your coworkers, you go home and relieve the baby-sitter. You may not be happy about giving up your fun, but you do—sometimes kicking and screaming—for the good of your marriage and family.

You may not say you are sacrificing for love. But that's the reason you do it: because of love. Your marriage is more important to you than a night out or a weekend game. You are living a life of love.

Father, marriage and family require sacrifices from both of us.
Give us the grace to accept this,
because sacrifice brings us closer and helps us grow as a family.

Some days it's hard to accept that God made us just the way He wanted us. Ask the woman struggling into a pair of jeans that have suddenly become one size too small, or the man who was passed over for promotion because the guy at the next desk graduated from Harvard. Our limitations are all too apparent, especially to ourselves, and we often wonder why God issued all these built-in insufficiencies, let alone blessed them.

> So God created man
> in his own image,
> in the image of God he created him;
> male and female he created them.
> God blessed them.
> GENESIS 1:27–28 NIV

Yet God doesn't have bad days or lapses in judgment. We have to assume we are exactly what we were meant to be and go on from there. Some things we can improve on, some things we can't. The one thing we can always do is accept God's blessing, just as we are.

Father, we can't always understand why we are what we are,
but we know You have a plan for our lives and will bring that plan to completion,
no matter how limited we seem to be.

> Many a man claims to
> have unfailing love,
> but a faithful man who can find?
> PROVERBS 20:6 NIV

Is your love for your spouse perfect? Do you always act out of unfailing love? Of course not, you're human. Sometimes you speak sharply to your spouse, ignore your children, stomp out of the house in anger, or shut it all out in front of the TV. Anyone who expects unfailing love will probably have that notion dispelled before the honeymoon's over. Unfailing love belongs in songs and dreams, not in real life.

But that doesn't mean we should never love. How foolish it would be to look for the "perfect" mate when we ourselves are so imperfect. Instead of looking for the imperfections, concentrate on your mate's good qualities, the things that made you fall in love in the first place. Praise those qualities and thank God for bringing you together, imperfections and all.

Father, neither of us is perfect, and our love is a flawed human love.
When we have problems, let us look to You as the example of perfect love we should aim for,
even though we know we'll fall far short of the mark.

One generation will commend
your works to another;
they will tell of your mighty acts.
PSALM 145:4 NIV

Parents and grandparents have the duty of passing knowledge on to their children and grandchildren, whether the younger generations want to hear from them or not. At times, this is more burdensome for the young than for their elders. They don't seem to care that Aunt Matilda was a missionary or Uncle George pulled a whole family out of a burning house thirty years ago.

But elders plug on because there are valuable lessons to be learned from the past. And in time the young begin to appreciate those little stories in ways that tend to overwhelm their elders. They ask to hear them again, they delight in old photos of ugly people in ugly clothing, and they even have been known to name their own children after a long-gone relative!

Lord, every family has its heroes, and our children need to know them,
even if only from our stories, because they act as models of godly behavior.
When we become elders ourselves,
help us pass on what we have heard to the next generation.

> I am the vine,
> ye are the branches:
> He that abideth in me, and I in him,
> the same bringeth forth much fruit:
> for without me ye can do nothing.
> JOHN 15:5 KJV

We all go through dry periods in life when we feel totally unproductive. We may be stuck in a dead-end job, unable to make progress on any front. We're like the branches we prune from our foundation plants, ready for the compost heap. At least they'll serve a purpose as compost.

Some of these discouraging periods are mercifully short, but others can go on for a long time. How do you cope with them? All you can do is cling to the Lord, your vine, and know that somehow, someday, you will be fruitful and accomplish His purpose for your life. Until then, it's your job to hang in there with all your might and live in faith and hope.

Lord, when these dry periods hit us, fill us with Your presence.
Hang onto us tightly until we mature enough to bear the fruit You have designed us to bear.

_____
_____
_____
_____
_____
_____
_____
_____
_____
_____
_____
_____

Notice the progression in this verse. *Rise* for the aged; show *respect* for the elderly; *revere* your God. Everything is in proportion.

> Rise in the presence of the aged, show respect for the elderly and revere your God.
> LEVITICUS 19:32 NIV

Common courtesy requires that we stand when a person older than ourselves approaches, even if he or she is not very old. The elderly, on the other hand, deserve our respect just because they have survived so long and must know more than we do. We may not revere them, but we respect them.

God, however, we rise for, show respect for, *and* revere.

Father, help us show the proper amount of deference to those older and wiser than ourselves,
no matter how we may personally feel about them,
and help us teach our children to do likewise. May we always revere You,
our God forever and ever.

Today is Mother's Day, a day for family celebrations. From cards to telephone calls to flowers to a family dinner out, it doesn't much matter what is planned, as long as something is. While most mothers will claim that absolutely nothing is required of their children—they'll cook dinner for whoever shows up—make sure a plan is in the works.

Now is a good time to look ahead, though. What will *you* want when your children are grown and gone and Mother's Day rolls around? Once a tradition is set, it's hard to change. If you want all the kids at your place when you're old, maybe you'd better show up at your parents' place today. You do reap what you sow.

Sometimes being a Christian makes you stand out like a sore thumb. Consider a scene at a fast-food restaurant. If your family routinely says grace before meals at home, your children are going to squirm in their seats at the restaurant, especially if you are sitting near their friends. You know you can't abandon the practice without giving your children the message that faith should be compromised in public for fear of embarrassment. You may have to make a few adjustments in volume or length, but giving in totally teaches the wrong lesson.

If ye were of the world, the world would love his own: but because ye are not of the world, but I have chosen you out of the world, therefore the world hateth you.

JOHN 15:19 KJV

Father, society may not actually hate us when we demonstrate our faith, but it certainly isn't supportive of our way of life. In such moments, give us the strength we need to bring our children up in the faith.

_____ TUESDAY _____

> Sow to yourselves in
> righteousness, reap in mercy;
> break up your fallow ground:
> for it is time to seek the LORD,
> till he come and rain
> righteousness upon you.
>
> HOSEA 10:12 KJV

The first step is always ours, and it's always difficult. If you have decided to follow the Lord, you need to begin living according to His commandments. Where you start is up to you, but once you start, you can't hold anything back. Your whole life has to be committed. So, you begin living righteously, and it's hard work. Sometimes it is so hard you find yourself backsliding a little now and then.

The good news is that in time it becomes easier. As you feel closer and closer to the Lord, you become more secure in your actions. Finally, you feel God "raining" His righteousness and mercy upon you instead of having to struggle for every little victory on your own.

Lord, we know living righteously is a lifetime pursuit,
but we have Your Word as our guide and
will not give up when the journey becomes difficult.

Along with righteousness comes temptation; the two seem locked in a perpetual circle. Temptation shakes the foundations of righteousness, and when temptation is overcome, the victory strengthens righteousness.

Don't get too smug, though. In a time of victory, another temptation is sure to be lurking just around the bend. This is a lifetime battle that will never go away, given our sinful nature. James tells us that enduring temptations can actually lead to blessings for those who suffer and overcome them. Those who love the Lord will prevail, with His help.

> Blessed is the man that endureth temptation: for when he is tried, he shall receive the crown of life, which the Lord hath promised to them that love him.
> JAMES 1:12 KJV

Father, it's hard to overcome the temptations of life, but we can,
because You are beside us in good times and bad,
and Your strength is enough for us.

> For we have not an high priest which cannot be touched with the feeling of our infirmities; but was in all points tempted like as we are, yet without sin.
> HEBREWS 4:15 KJV

God knows all there is to know about temptation, and more than we'll ever need to know ourselves. Our Judge has been on the streets and down in the muck, tempted by the devil himself, the all-time expert at temptation. He dealt with it all and never stumbled, which is more than we can say, but He knows very well how hard the struggle can be.

The next time you are struggling with temptation and feel yourself sinking into the mud, reach out your hand and ask the Lord to pull you up. He knows how you feel. He's been there.

Lord, it's so good to know that You, our Judge,
understand the difficulty of life and the quagmire of temptation.
Hear our pleas when we call out to You for help,
for we know You will have mercy.

Some wise person once noted that old age is not for sissies. Aging brings a whole new set of challenges that couples must learn to deal with, including the fear of abandonment. Neither of you is the same person you were thirty years ago. Hair goes gray or away, muscles migrate south, and you begin to fear you are no longer physically attractive to your spouse. Even though you trust your partner, you know you could never compete with a "youngster" of forty.

> Cast me not off in the time of old age; forsake me not when my strength faileth.
> PSALM 71:9 KJV

Well, your spouse has the same worries! If you've made it this far as a couple, your worries are most likely unfounded. Take time to reassure your spouse that your love has not lessened, just matured.

Father, help us adjust to our aging bodies and put away any fears we may have about our attractiveness, and remind us to reassure each other of our love.

The Lord knoweth how to deliver the godly out of temptations.
2 PETER 2:9 KJV

Have you been trying to save yourself from temptation through your own willpower? Has it been working? That piece of chocolate cake was stronger than you. That movie you rented took you places you don't want to be and you're not sure you can get back. That lie at work fooled the boss. It was so good it even fooled you for a while.

Willpower won't do the job. Willpower is just you, a stronger, more determined you, maybe, but still just a normal, weak human being. Willpower has its limits. You need to call in the reserves. Don't you believe that the Lord who saved your soul is perfectly capable of helping you turn away from sin? Just ask Him. He knows how to deliver you.

Lord, sometimes we get so involved in saving ourselves—
in self-improvement, empowerment, and all the current fads—
that we forget You are more than willing to help.
Help us see our own lack of ability and accept the gifts You give so readily.

We've been wallowing around in temptation for a few days, so why not take a closer look? Understanding the enemy is always a good defense. Dig out your concordance and begin looking up some verses about correction, guilt, lust, lying, mercy, obedience, repentance, sexual sins, sin, and temptation. Then pick out one verse that speaks most directly to the fight you are fighting, write it down, and hang it on the refrigerator for a week (especially helpful if you have a problem with gluttony!).

The glory of young men
is their strength:
and the beauty of old men
is the grey head.
PROVERBS 20:29 KJV

Why would a man even think of dyeing his gray hair? He should be delighted just to *have hair*. Besides, most women "of a certain age" find gray hair extremely attractive on a man. Such a man is seen as experienced, stable, and wise, all admirable qualities.

There is much to be said for aging gracefully, for being free to be whoever you are at this stage of life.

Lord, help me accept myself as I am today and not try to look
like a twenty-year-old when I'm fifty.
You made me what I am, and I thank You for my gray head.

Being a grandparent is one of God's rewards for hanging in there and, at times, putting up with your children. Sure, you love your children, but they were, and always will be, a responsibility. Along with the joy they brought you came duties, worries, and obligations. With them, you had to do the right thing, day after day, for over twenty years.

> Children's children are the crown of old men.
> PROVERBS 17:6 KJV

Grandchildren, on the other hand, are pure, unadulterated joy. They expect nothing of you, and when you get tired, you can send them home. You can buy them expensive toys without worrying about spoiling them. When they ask difficult questions, you may be surprised to discover that you actually know the answers. They will love you if you fall asleep in the middle of their bedtime story, laugh at your stupidest joke, and be happy to see you whenever you appear on their doorstep.

And there is yet another benefit: All the emotional baggage between you and your children is thrown away the minute you see your first grandchild.

Lord, our grandchildren are a taste of immortality to come,
and we thank You for blessing us with their presence.

That the aged men be
sober, grave, temperate,
sound in faith,
in charity, in patience.
TITUS 2:2 KJV

Like it or not, once men reach a certain stage in life, they are expected to be good examples. One would hardly look to a teenager for guidance, after all, and men involved in bringing up their own children don't have the time or patience to be good examples to anyone else. But you learn a lot as time goes by. Life slows down when the kids leave home, and you know it's time to pass on some of your knowledge to the next generation. The easiest and most effective way to do this is to show others how it's supposed to be done.

This should not be a frightening chore for anyone. No, you're not perfect, and no, you don't have all the answers, but you do have some of them. Why not share them?

Lord, no one who really knows me would say I'm a good example.
You know my failings.
But I'm willing to try, and with Your guidance and support,
maybe I can be helpful to someone else.

The last time you had to write a check for your federal taxes, did you notice that instead of making it payable to the Internal Revenue Service you now pay the U.S. Treasury? It may be just a public relations ploy on the part of the government, but it's a good one. We've all been promoted and now report to someone higher, which somehow makes writing that check a little easier.

> Labour not to be rich;
> cease from thine own wisdom.
> Wilt thou set thine eyes upon
> that which is not?
> for riches certainly make
> themselves wings;
> they fly away as
> an eagle toward heaven.
> PROVERBS 23:4–5 KJV

We have the option of reporting to a higher authority in all financial matters. Each couple decides how to handle their own finances: how much to spend, save, invest, and donate. Very few of us will ever be rich, but we all set our own priorities. Are yours in line with your beliefs?

Father, help us handle our finances according to Your wishes,
for You are our ultimate authority.

FRIDAY

> A little that
> a righteous man hath
> is better than the riches
> of many wicked.
> PSALM 37:16 KJV

The Bible has nothing against money itself: Money isn't evil, but the desire for it can make us evil. We cut moral corners to save or gain a few dollars, putting money ahead of righteousness. We cheat our spouses and children of the time and attention they need in order to get that next promotion, saying we will work fewer hours once we get it. But once we're there, there is another peak to climb.

How are your priorities today? Do you know when to say "enough"? Are you strong enough to earn your salary with righteousness and be satisfied with what you have when getting more becomes a burden to those you love?

Father, there comes a time when we have enough to live on and a little left over to enjoy. When it's time to stop pushing, or when our desire for more gets out of hand, teach us how to be satisfied with what we have.

Men are not the only ones told to serve as examples of godly living. Women have strengths of their own —such wonderful resources as compassion, fidelity, and love—that need to be taught to the next generation. Because of their role as mother, many women shy away from directly teaching but instead teach through their actions in the church and community. Their seemingly tireless dedication to others is enough to show the depth of their faith and encourages others to pitch in with them.

> The aged women likewise, that they be in behaviour as becometh holiness, not false accusers, not given to much wine, teachers of good things.
> TITUS 2:3 KJV

Whether they organize church fairs, bake a pie for the bake sale, or single-handedly keep the Sunday school running, women have much to teach the community.

Father, I have no great talent to share, but I do have time to invest.
Show me where I am needed the most.

Couples tend to develop friendships with other couples of the same age. This Sunday, why not bridge the generation gap a bit? If your church has a social hour after services, introduce yourselves to a couple from another age group, either older or younger. Let them know that you admire the work they do for the church, chat for a while, and then seek out another couple. You may be surprised how many charming, talented people you can meet in less than an hour.

The Jewish people end their Passover feast with the words, "Next year in Jerusalem." Every year, through pogroms, persecutions, and horrors of all kinds, Jews around the world have held onto the hope of celebrating their next Passover in Jerusalem. They know, more than most, that "the expectation of the poor shall not perish for ever."

> For the needy shall not alway be forgotten: the expectation of the poor shall not perish for ever.
> PSALM 9:18 KJV

A Christian couple must be able to sustain the same level of hope in their lives, no matter what their current situation. It's not easy when you're playing Russian roulette with the monthly bills or have to send a brilliant child to a trade school instead of the university he or she deserves. But there is always hope.

Father, we know You can work things out for us.
In the meantime, give us hope.

There is that maketh himself rich,
yet hath nothing:
there is that maketh himself poor,
yet hath great riches.
PROVERBS 13:7 KJV

What do you consider riches? That's the question every couple has to answer for themselves. Would you lose your spouse and children for the sake of your bank balance, or would you give every penny to keep them with you? If paying your tithe means not paying off your credit card bill, which do you choose? If hiring a tutor to get a child through physics means no vacation, what is your pleasure?

Decisions like these hammer at us unmercifully, day after day. The big ones are pretty easy to figure out, but some of the little ones are tricky. Dinner out or rice and beans at home? Fix the car's transmission or straighten the child's teeth?

The choice is yours.

Father, every decision we make is important.
Help us decide where our true riches are and set our priorities in accordance with Your wishes.

You say you don't have much in common with Bill Gates? After all, he could buy and sell your whole town, while you can barely pay the electricity bill run up by a computer. Yet if you can get past the financial gulf, he's not all that different. He has a wife and family, just like you do. He undoubtedly gets headaches and an upset stomach every now and then. He wears glasses because his eyes aren't perfect, and he pays taxes like everyone else (only more so).

All of us, rich or poor, have more in common than we think. The Lord made us all. As the proverbial relative would say, "He puts his pants on one leg at a time, just like me."

> The rich and poor meet together:
> the LORD is the maker of them all.
> PROVERBS 22:2 KJV

Father, instead of seeing only our differences,
help us see what we have in common and treat everyone as Your children.

> Riches profit
> not in the day of wrath:
> but righteousness
> delivereth from death.
> PROVERBS 11:4 KJV

There's no bank in heaven, and even if there were, you'd still arrive at the so-called pearly gates empty-handed. God doesn't care how much cash you leave behind. You did what you did with your life, and money is just part of what you did.

The next time you have to make a life decision, take a minute to think about how that decision will affect your future. Riches can't give you eternal life, but Jesus can and will.

Father, thank You for sending Your Son, Jesus,
to redeem us from our sins and wash them away.

Both of you may work full-time outside the home, or one may work full-time while the other cares for the house and family, but no matter what your working arrangement, your wealth and security don't come from an employer. Likewise, if you own your own business, you shouldn't pin your hopes on this year's profit.

> Ask the Lord for rain in the springtime; it is the Lord who makes the storm clouds. He gives showers of rain to men, and plants of the field to everyone.
> ZECHARIAH 10:1 NIV

No business has the answers to every problem. Indeed, no employer can promise happiness, rid you of incurable illness, or provide rain in the midst of a drought. Money can only solve so much. It's a helpful tool, but not a god.

God provides all the solutions for our lives, whether it's rain to bring relief to a parched land or arid, clear days that dry out a wet home. He heals unhappy relationships and can cure illnesses doctors can't even identify.

All we have to do is ask and trust in Him.

Our trust is in You, Jesus, not our jobs or businesses.
Thank You for providing for our every need.

If we were starting a missions project, we would not send missionaries off without a penny. We'd spend months, or even years, making sure we had the funds to start well.

> Provide neither gold, nor silver, nor brass in your purses.
> MATTHEW 10:9 KJV

But Jesus sent the twelve disciples out to share the Gospel carrying flat purses, dependent on God and the people to whom they preached. *How could such men prosper?* we may wonder. Yet those twelve penniless men reached a nation.

Money, slick advertisements, and careful plans aren't what it takes to spread the Gospel of Jesus Christ. Belief in God is the critical element. Though faithful giving to groups with ambitious goals is not wrong, we need to recognize that money doesn't run the organization, God does. Where He blesses obedience, provision appears for those who go and those who organize.

Without money, a missions project might face difficulty. Without God, it has no purpose at all.

Whatever mission we give to, Lord, we understand that You provide for it. When we reach out to others, keep our eyes off our pocketbooks and firmly on You.

God has provided for you in many ways: a job, a home, and food for each day. Even if you don't dine on filet mignon, you have a full stomach.

Spend time thanking God for His provision and lifting up needs to Him.

Many good missions need support. Some need money, while others need physical help. Talk to your pastor and other leaders about those they would recommend, or learn from friends what their experiences have been. Identify a mission you would like to help and choose a way in which you can assist. You may choose to support a child in a Third World country, help out at a soup kitchen, or write to and pray for missionaries whom your church already supports.

Supporting a mission is a matter of faith, not cash.

> Thy word is
> a lamp unto my feet,
> and a light unto my path.
> PSALM 119:105 KJV

God's Word lights your path and shows you the way to go. Not reading God's Word is like taking a candle into the dark without lighting the wick. You'll stumble over anything in the road.

Have you read through the *whole* Bible together? If not, you risk bumbling around spiritually and stubbing your toes on obstacles Satan throws in your way. Your shared light may burn dimly or even nearly go out.

Don't read Scripture on anyone else's time schedule; rather, make it a natural part of your day together. Whether you open the Book together before you start your day or cuddle up in bed with it before you turn out the light, read it.

Once you've finished, start again. After all, just because you used a lamp to light your way one night doesn't mean you can see in the dark. And the light of Scripture burns brighter all the time, as you stow it away in your heart and live by its glow.

Thank You, Lord, for the brightness of Your Word.
Let it shine out to others as we read and share it day by day.

_____

_____

_____

_____

_____

_____

_____

_____

_____

_____

_____

_____

_____

When a book is supposed to be the "last word" on a subject, it's often called a bible. You can find bibles on home repair, cooking, and other how-to subjects. Each aims to give you excellent advice.

> I rejoice at Your word
> as one who finds great treasure.
> PSALM 119:162 NKJV

From these volumes you may learn to fix a leaky faucet or cook a tasty meal, but you won't find valuable advice on how to live better, heal wounded relationships, or gain eternal life.

God's Word doesn't just show us how to do something well. Scripture wraps itself around our hearts and fills our lives, changing our way of thinking and our actions. Reading God's Word turns us into new people whose hearts are focused on Him.

Look to a cooking bible for life advice, and you'll get burned, but look to the Scriptures, and you'll find a "great treasure." It will support you forever.

Now *that's* the last Word.

Thank You, Lord God, for giving us Your Word on every subject.
Let us treat it as the great treasure it is.

> But be doers of the word,
> not hearers only,
> deceiving yourselves.
> JAMES 1:22 NKJV

Suppose you walked down the aisle with a member of the opposite sex, spoke the words that made you man and wife, and never lived with that person. How many people would believe you had a real, close relationship?

We wouldn't think of doing such a thing to a person, but many of us do just that to God. We walk down an aisle, claim His Name, but live as if we have no obligations.

Not doing what God calls you to do is like a marriage without commitment: It's not much of a relationship. Because you never followed through on the words you spoke at the altar, you'd find it hard to explain to others that you really loved your spouse. Similarly, commit yourself to Christ and fail to do what He says, and even non-Christians will easily spot your lack of devotion.

If you really love God, don't only read His Word—follow through on it, too. Then the world will know you're committed, and you won't deceive anyone—least of all yourself.

*Lord, teach us not to deceive ourselves but to love You with all our hearts
and have a complete commitment to acting out Your Word.*

Life's crushing us. We didn't follow God's Word because the solution seemed so obvious. With only the best of intentions, we wandered off His path. Now stuck in a swamp of sin, we desperately need help.

> I cried unto thee;
> save me,
> and I shall keep thy testimonies.
> PSALM 119:146 KJV

We call out, "We'll be good, God, we promise. Just get us out of this!" And for those few seconds we mean it.

Crying out to God and admitting our sin are the right actions to take. As we feel ourselves slipping out of the swamp, His strong arms lifting us out of the muck, we know God keeps His promises. Soon God sets us back on course. He's kept His promises.

Unless we want to be more firmly stuck in that swamp, we must remember that mistake and keep our desperate promise, not forgetting it like some greedy child.

God's testimonies don't change. If we want to be like Him, ours shouldn't either.

Thank You, Father, for saving us from our own well-meaning efforts.
Cleanse us from sin today and keep us faithful to Your testimonies.

> Thou art near, O LORD;
> and all thy commandments
> are truth.
> PSALM 119:151 KJV

It's popular today to think that there is no truth, no absolute guidelines to follow. But those who tell you that simply have their own set of absolutes. Run headlong into them, and you'll discover what they are.

As Christians, we share truths God's Word established long ago. Others run headlong into those truths as we learn them and stand up for them. They may not agree or appreciate God's viewpoint, but they surely know what it is.

Being a witness to God's truth may not always be pleasant. Telling your rebellious child that she's making a serious mistake can seem hard. Speaking out on the truth of God's salvation may seem impossible in some family circumstances. But if you want the people you love to learn the truth and draw close to God, don't hold your tongue. Speak gently and considerately at an opportune time, but *do* speak.

We need to speak Your truth every day, Lord.
Keep us faithful to Your Word
so we know Your absolutes and can witness to them in our lives.

Oh, no, Bible study again. Instead of looking forward to it, we find Bible reading has become a chore.

> My lips shall utter praise, when thou hast taught me thy statutes.
> PSALM 119:171 KJV

Learning God's truths isn't meant to be spiritual drudgery, even when it's hard work. After all, we aren't aiming to start a marital competition to see who can memorize the most Bible verses! Knowing God's statutes should simply bring us to such appreciation of His nature that we burst into praise.

Stilted, worn-out phrases aren't praise, and anyone who tries to praise God that way misses the point: God's wonderful character has so blessed us that we can't stop talking about it. He has saved us, when once we had no care for Him or His truths; He has cleansed us of every sin and trusted us to share His truths with others in our families, workplaces, and world.

That kind of blessing rightly overflows from our lives, in all we say and do.

Lord, thank You for showing us Your love through your Word.
Let it overflow into our world through our praise.

God's Word wasn't meant to be shut up in your hearts. If it doesn't affect your actions, it isn't serving its best purpose.

This week, together, seek to share the truth of God's Word with a friend or family member. After praying about it, you may want to plan to get together with that person, write a joint note, or give a call.

Maybe your contact will share encouragement with a friend who's caring for a sick family member or struggling with personal problems. Perhaps it will introduce someone to the Good News that God's love applies to him.

There are many creative ways you can reach out together with God's truth. Plan to do that today.

Sometimes you "just know" what your spouse will think on a subject. He'll pass on an appetizer of mushrooms but never jumbo shrimp. She'll choose a vacation at the shore over one at the mountains.

> "But you, Israel, are My servant, Jacob, whom I have chosen, the descendants of Abraham My friend."
>
> ISAIAH 41:8 NKJV

You know what your mate feels and thinks because you've spent time together and discussed each other's likes and dislikes. You've become friends.

But do you "just know" what your friend Jesus likes and dislikes? Have you spent enough time with Him, through prayer and Bible reading, to have His opinion on the large and small events in life?

If not, you're acting like a servant, not a friend. You haven't drawn close enough to the Master to know that He offers you more than a job. He offers a *relationship* with Himself that beats any on earth.

Don't turn down that once-in-a-lifetime chance to cultivate an eternal relationship. Who would be servant to a Master who wants to be a Friend?

Jesus, our eternal friendship starts here on earth.
We offer You our service and our hearts.

_____ TUESDAY _____

A man of many companions
may come to ruin,
but there is a friend who
sticks closer than a brother.
PROVERBS 18:24 NIV

Before you knew Christ you might have had lots of friends—or very few. But if you chose your friends because they'd look good to the world, you were almost certainly disappointed. When you needed someone to help you, that help was probably scarce.

Christian friendships aren't a head count. No one, least of all God, judges people by the numbers of friends they have or don't have. God isn't in the counting business, and we shouldn't be either.

God's goal for friendships is depth, not number. A few close friendships—with other couples or singles—will support you in trouble when a multitude will fail you. One friend who stands with you is worth twenty who "just don't have time."

Whether you're giving to a friend or on the receiving end of help, the model you want to follow isn't what the world will think, but Jesus.

When it comes to friends, Jesus is the best one ever.

*Lord Jesus, help us to model all our friendships on You,
especially the one that makes up our marriage.*

Would you rethink your friendships, if you knew God were a witness between you?

Jonathan and David knew God was a third party to their friendship. So when Jonathan's father, King Saul, turned against his friend, Israel's prince helped David escape even though he knew he could face his father's wrath.

> Jonathan said to David,
> "Go in peace, for we have sworn friendship with each other in the name of the LORD, saying, 'The LORD is witness between you and me, and between your descendants and my descendants forever.'"
>
> 1 SAMUEL 20:42 NIV

When David became king, after his friend's death, Jonathan's son Mephibosheth might have been seen as an heir to Saul's throne. Yet David restored Saul's lands to Mephibosheth and honored him with a place at the new king's table (2 Samuel 9). It was no part of David's plan to eradicate his friend's family, as many new rulers would have done.

David's and Jonathan's relationship was not a convenient one that simply filled selfish needs. Can you and your spouse say the same of your friendships?

Lord, we want You to be a witness between us and our friends.
May our friendships reflect Your love.

> Wounds from a friend
> can be trusted,
> but an enemy multiplies kisses.
> PROVERBS 27:6 NIV

How could the person you love most say *that* about you? You thought your spouse was your best friend and now you wonder where that faithful friendship went. Wouldn't anyone rather have kisses than correction?

Criticism from a mate is usually not pleasant. After all, you value this person's opinion over all others. You want to please her or make him admire you.

But you know you're not perfect. None of us is. We all need to make personal changes, and it's a sign of love, not hate, for someone to kindly point out a midcourse correction that could keep your ship from being stranded on the rocks.

The person who just keeps kissing you and never says a word is your *real* enemy. Don't let the first sign of his or her true feelings be the grinding of rock on your keel.

*Lord, help us to be kind and gentle when we point out each other's weaknesses,
but help us to say the words that need to be spoken for the good of our marriage.*

_____

_____

_____

_____

_____

_____

_____

_____

_____

_____

_____

_____

_____

Perhaps you cannot imagine being unfaithful to your spouse. You would never hurt one who loves you and does so much for you.

> You adulterous people, don't you know that friendship with the world is hatred toward God? Anyone who chooses to be a friend of the world becomes an enemy of God.
>
> JAMES 4:4 NIV

But do you find it equally hard to think of hurting the One who loves you even more than your spouse? Is it easy to hurt God and not feel pain?

Your husband or wife shares a special, profound love with you, but God loves you even more deeply. No one else can take your place with Him, no matter how many people He saves. James compares turning away from His love with adultery.

Turning away from God and to the world separates you from Him as surely as turning to another member of the opposite sex parts you from your mate.

Today, choose whom you'll love: Jesus or the world.

*Lord, You've shown us so much love, yet how easily we turn from You.
Keep our hearts near You and part us from the world's temptations.*

"Greater love has no one than this,
that he lay down his life for his friends.
You are my friends if
you do what I command."
JOHN 15:13–14 NIV

Jesus showed His love for us by His great sacrifice. The innocent One took on all our sins and died on the cross that we might live. Who among even our best friends would do such a thing for us? The Lord of the universe wanted to bring us back to Himself so badly that He died to do it.

Coming to know Jesus is priceless but not free. He paid the cost of our sin, but if we treat that lightly, we show we don't understand its worth. Nothing on earth could buy His friendship, yet all He asks of us is simple obedience. Our submission to His will shows we don't hold His life cheap.

Divine friendship that came at no sacrifice would be cheap, not priceless.

Such love as You have offered us, Lord Jesus, can only be answered by our hearts.
We give You our love and seek to show it through obedience to Your Word.

_____

_____

_____

_____

_____

_____

_____

_____

_____

_____

_____

_____

_____

_____

_____

_____

_____

_____

Friendship has a certain amount of reciprocity to it. To be a friend, you have to share time or help others.

Prepare a time of help or sharing with one friend or a number of them. Invite a single friend to share an after-church pizza or plan a dinner party for a few couples. Or you might consider babysitting for a friend who needs time away from her kids or lending a hand helping a friend with home repairs.

As you plan, think about the things that make your friendship with Jesus special. How can you show His love for others though your relationships?

You may also want to tell your friend what makes your relationship so special. Most of us don't speak often to our nonbelieving friends of those feelings, and we often feel embarrassed when we do begin to share our faith. Think of encouraging, positive words and then speak them from your heart.

> Oh, that I had in the desert
> a lodging place for travelers,
> so that I might leave my people
> and go away from them;
> for they are all adulterers,
> a crowd of unfaithful people.
>
> JEREMIAH 9:2 NIV

Have you ever wanted to run away from home? When daily pressures lean on you, solitude seems most appealing.

The prophet Jeremiah knew how you feel. He wanted to run away from his "job" of telling the people how far they were from God and visit a desert resort.

Every marriage has moments when each member needs some space. An hour or two might help, if you need to think out some things. Or maybe you're tired and need some serious nap time. But don't make that a long parting or you'll risk increasing the emotional distance between you.

Though Jeremiah was irritated and even disgusted by his people, he didn't give up on them. One word from the Lord and he was on the spot again.

Take a break, but don't break with God or your spouse.

Lord, when we need space,
help us to be gracious about it and return to each other refreshed.

Naomi had reason to grieve. Her husband and sons had died in Moab and now Naomi was alone, except for Ruth, one of her daughters-in-law, who refused to forsake her, and had accompanied her to Judah. Naomi's lot certainly seemed hard and hopeless. She was right when she said she'd gone out full and come home empty.

> "I went out full, but the LORD has brought me back empty."
> RUTH 1:21 NASB

But God had blessed Naomi in ways she couldn't imagine. Ruth would be part of the "solution" to make Naomi full again. Through one faithful woman, Naomi would experience the birth of her grandson, Obed. Again, she would feel blessed.

Have you gone out full and come back empty? Perhaps you've made unwise decisions that are affecting your marriage. Maybe you've fallen into sin and are working your way out of its results. You've turned to God for help, but rescue hasn't been quick in coming.

Don't fall prey to bitterness. God isn't finished with your life yet. In His perfect timing, you'll go out full again.

Lord, we know Your filling.
Today, whether we are full or empty, we trust in You.

> With praise and thanksgiving
> they sang to the LORD:
> "He is good;
> his love to Israel endures forever."
> And all the people gave a great shout
> of praise to the LORD because
> the foundation of the house
> of the LORD was laid.
>
> EZRA 3:11 NIV

As the Israelites began rebuilding their temple, they had an easy time praising God. Joy came naturally as they saw His hand at work.

Thanking God and telling of His wonders is a snap when you're on a spiritual high. But every Christian couple has times when it's hard to see God's "kingdom building" in their lives. Perhaps a loved one dies, or the ministry that started so prosperously faces rough patches. Suddenly praise becomes difficult.

Is the same God who told the Israelites to build the temple still in control of the universe? Is He still good? Or has one of your life circumstances changed His nature?

God does not change; God always deserves praise. Today give Him your richest sacrifice as you glorify Him, despite life's challenges.

No matter what challenges we face today, Jesus,
You are still the mighty Lord of our lives.
We delight in Your grace and love.

Sargon, the king of Assyria, sent people of many nations to resettle Samaria. When lions began to attack them, he sent a priest along. The pagan king figured Samaria's deity was angry and needed placating.

> Nevertheless,
> each national group made its own gods
> in the several towns where they settled,
> and set them up in the shrines
> the people of Samaria had made
> at the high places.
> 2 KINGS 17:29 NIV

But the new Samaritans would never really understand Yahweh or what He required. They had toted along their own idols, set up shrines, and worshiped them, along with Yahweh. They imagined that no one would be offended and that everyone could be happy.

Instead they ended up with a religious mess and found themselves despised by faithful Jews and spiritually empty.

Although we don't set figurines up in our homes and bow down to them, we may become idol worshipers in more sophisticated ways. We placate unbelievers instead of sharing our faith. We accept non-Christian practices without a blink of the eye. Suddenly we're in a mess and we wonder how we got there.

Maybe we slid down the path to Samaria.

Lord, we don't want to live in unfaithfulness.
Make our hearts and lips devoted to You.

> The Samaritan woman
> said to him [Jesus],
> "You are a Jew and
> I am a Samaritan woman.
> How can you ask me for a drink?"
> (For Jews do not associate
> with Samaritans.)
> JOHN 4:9 NIV

King Sargon had sent non-Jews into Samaria when he resettled the area, and the Jews had never forgotten or forgiven his action. The Samaritans had the wrong background and a syncretistic faith that only partly worshiped God.

No question about it, Jesus knew He wasn't confronting the model believer when He spoke to the Samaritan woman. But He didn't look at her forebears, her theology, or even her sin. Nor did He cave in when she pointed out the differences in faith between her people and His.

We face similar situations with coworkers, friends, and family members. Both outwardly "good" people and "sinners" think they've learned about God and don't like what they've seen. Their broken lives reflect that.

We can add to their false perceptions or, like Jesus, go beyond them, to show what God is really like. We can bring heat or light to our discussions.

But only light will change hearts.

Help us reach out to those who have only been inoculated with a weak knowledge of You, Lord. We want to be a testimony to real faith.

_____

_____

_____

_____

_____

_____

_____

_____

_____

_____

_____

No one has 20/20 vision when it comes to seeing God's plans. He doesn't let us view everything ahead of time, because then our "faith vision" would never increase.

> He withdraweth not his eyes from the righteous.
> JOB 36:7 KJV

Like Job, when our vision is obscured by difficult times, we may wonder if God has overlooked us. As Job's body became covered with sores and this faithful man lost those he loved, his struggles were hard to bear. Then his three "friends" stopped by with "advice" that only made his situation worse.

Elihu, one of the supposed friends, did make one good point: God hadn't missed Job's troubles. No blind eye was turned toward his trials. God cared deeply.

God cares when we, too, face troubles that seem to overwhelm us. Our sores may be emotional, not physical, but His 20/20 vision hasn't missed them.

Though we may not preview God's plans, we can still trust that they exist. All we need are eyes of faith.

Lord, we need clear vision to trust during trials.
Let our faith see, even when our eyes don't.

Not much faith is necessary when life is business as usual. You may know what to expect most days from your home life, a comfortable job, or a church you've gone to for years.

What will challenge you to leave a business-as-usual life and take some risks for God? Perhaps you need to volunteer to support a missions project with time or funds, develop a plan for a new faith venture, or witness to someone who has been on your heart for a long time.

Begin to plan through prayer. If you want to support a mission, should it be an overseas one or something in your own backyard? How much support should you offer? If you need to develop something new, whom should you invite to share the work with you? Or can you handle it alone, as a couple? God can direct you to answer these questions. To witness to a friend, pray that God will guide you in your speech and your testimony of caring.

If you need to develop additional plans, remember that God's eye does not leave you. Determine to remain faithful through every stage and to bring all your concerns before Him.

The Israelites had seen their lives destroyed by a foreign, pagan people before they were carried off as slaves to Babylon. Now God's people were poor in heart and spirit, as well as financially. For them, good news didn't seem to exist.

> The LORD has anointed me to preach good news to the poor. He has sent me to bind up the brokenhearted, to proclaim freedom for the captives and release from darkness for the prisoners.
>
> ISAIAH 61:1 NIV

God didn't rush in and change the circumstances for His disobedient people. But they wouldn't always be brokenhearted captives, sitting in darkness. God promised that someday He would free them, not just from physical bondage but from sin that had caused this situation in the first place.

We may not be chained slaves, dragged to a foreign land, but we feel the weight of spiritual and emotional chains in our marriage. Today God still offers us freedom and release from darkness.

Have you walked out into the light of His Good News?

Lord Jesus, thank You for freeing us from sin.
When its chains seek to wrap around us, we turn to You to break their strength.

> I will heal their backsliding,
> I will love them freely:
> for mine anger is
> turned away from him.
> HOSEA 14:4 KJV

How easy to slide into sin, and how hard to break away from it!

Turning away from sin means a serious fight against temptation. You grasp your spiritual weapons and charge into the fray. But just when you feel you've made real headway, you run smack against the same sin. Is God angry with you? Will you ever have victory?

God may let you fight sin for a while. Perhaps you need to learn its cost, so you'll evade it another time. But keep on avoiding that sin, fighting back with God's Word, and seeking to do right, and it *will* become a thing of the past.

The pain of separation from God felt so sharp when you disobeyed Him. God felt angry and distant. But as you waged battle, you began to understand how much He hated the sin that kept you from Him. You felt His love return.

As His healing filled your being, you stood firm against temptation. You slid back where you should be.

Thank You, Lord, for keeping us from sin.
Turn us from it each day so we may rejoice in Your love.

Jesus makes us truly free. When we first believe in Him, we may feel swept clean of sin. How wonderful it is to have all the cobwebs dusted from our spirits!

> "If you abide in My word, then you are truly disciples of Mine; and you shall know the truth, and the truth shall make you free."
> JOHN 8:31–32 NASB

But if we follow that new life with wrong deeds, those cobwebs pile up again, and we're more aware of them than ever. Now we *really* know what grungy feels like.

Jesus frees us from sin, but we don't stay liberated long if we ignore the truths of His Word. He didn't provide us with a new lifestyle to have us slip back into wrongdoing. Instead, He gave us specific ways to avoid sin.

True disciples don't try to see how much sin they can "get away with." They know God freed them for a purpose, and it wasn't to see how far they could go.

Lord Jesus, thank You for providing us with such freedom.
We want to obey Your Word and fulfill Your purpose for our lives.

Week 26

> But now having been freed from sin and enslaved to God, you derive your benefit, resulting in sanctification, and the outcome, eternal life.
> ROMANS 6:22 NASB

Loosed from sin, you become not a free agent, who runs his or her own life, but a slave of God. There is no third option; you serve God or Satan.

Slavery to God is nothing like slavery to sin. Where once you did wrong, no matter how hard you struggled, now you do right, though not perfectly. Every day you become more and more like Jesus. Instead of bondage, freedom from sin rules your soul, and love replaces hatred in your heart. That can't help but improve your marriage.

You may not be a perfect mate, but if you walk closely with God, as you become more like Him, you'll be more caring and forgiving. Both you and your spouse will see faith's benefits.

Yet God has even more in store for you—eternal life together with Him.

Such freedom as You offer, Lord, cannot be found in sin.
Thank You for making us free in all things.

All we could earn, out of our own efforts, was death. Hard as we tried, nothing could clean us up enough to approach the Holy One. Seeing our filthy, disgusting rags, who could blame Him for excluding us from His holy heaven?

> For the wages of sin is death, but the free gift of God is eternal life in Christ Jesus our Lord.
> ROMANS 6:23 NASB

We had it all wrong, though. Earning brownie points or saving up enough good deeds wouldn't get us into heaven. God had a free gift prepared for us, one He wanted to place in our hands. But we turned away.

God shows us what free is really like by giving a lavish gift we could never hope to afford. But He doesn't stop there. This gift is not only valuable for this life alone but also draws us into never-ending days, shared with Him.

All this, simply for opening our arms and hearts to accept the greatest gift available in time or eternity: Jesus.

We open our arms to You each day, Jesus.
Give us freedom to share Your gift with the world.

"If you knew the gift of God. . .
He would have given you
living water."
JOHN 4:10 NASB

Have you ever tried to give someone a gift and been turned down? It wasn't easy, was it? It didn't make you feel good, and perhaps, for a while, you felt miffed. After all, you were trying to do something good for that person. You wanted to show your love.

But you can't force a gift on anyone. Those who won't accept it simply go "giftless."

God offers the gift of eternal life, but many reject it. Caught up in sin, like the Samaritan woman, they can't even see what's being offered. If they know about God, they think He's some distant force that would never offer *them* a gift. They may talk about theology, yet the living water doesn't flow through their hearts.

But one day their lives catch up to them. Miserable and alone, they turn, see the Giver, and hold out their hands.

Suddenly, living water washes through their souls.

Lord, we've tried to share Your gift of love with others and have been turned down.
Don't let that pain keep us from reaching out again.

It's almost time for vacation and all the planning that involves. But before you make the usual reservations at the usual location, see if your "vacation requirements" have changed in the past year. Would your children prefer a week at the shore to the usual vacation at the lake? Is it time for that trip to Disney World? Will your finances finally allow a cruise, or would a week with relatives be more affordable and just as much fun? Take time to discuss your vacation with the whole family and try to please as many members as possible within your budget. The years for family vacations go by quickly, so make them as memorable as possible.

_____ MONDAY _____

All hard work brings a profit,
but mere talk leads only to poverty.
PROVERBS 14:23 NIV

Some days the world seems divided into two class-
es: those who actually do the work and those who
talk about it. Every business needs a certain
amount of planning and oversight if it is to grow
and prosper. But a company of all chiefs and no war-
riors eventually will plan itself right out of business.

The same is true of families. We all know that retirement planning is essential these days, but what's the point of planning how to invest your money if there is no money to invest? One way or another, we all have to get down in the ditches and do the hard work that brings a profit. Then, as our profits accumulate, we can plan how to use them.

*Lord, give us patience as we do the hard work that
will lead us to financial security in the future.*

We spend years teaching our children, correcting them, and, oh yes, worrying about them (a hard habit to break). Then one day they surprise us and grow into wonderful, capable adults.

But it is the spirit in a man, the breath of the Almighty, that gives him understanding. It is not only the old who are wise, not only the aged who understand what is right.
JOB 32:8–9 NIV

Of course a good part of this comes from the way we raised them, and this should give us joy. But much of their wisdom comes from within themselves, from their spirit, their own hard-won understanding. Don't feel unneeded or abandoned when your children show unexpected maturity. Rejoice!

Father, give our children Your guidance throughout their lives. We cannot raise them properly on our own. We need Your help.

"What is this you are doing?"
they asked.
"Are you rebelling
against the king?"
NEHEMIAH 2:19 NIV

Today we celebrate our independence and the freedom it gives us to disagree, to make our opinions known without fear, and to take part in governing ourselves as a free people. The same freedoms should be an integral part of family life.

All family members need to feel free to voice their opinions and have them taken into consideration. True, parents have the final word in many matters, but even a small child needs the freedom to speak his or her mind without fear, to "rebel against the king," and sometimes to win.

Lord, You are the King of our family, not us.
Help us give our children the encouragement they need to grow
into intelligent adults not afraid to speak their minds.

_____

_____

_____

_____

_____

_____

_____

_____

_____

_____

_____

_____

_____

When we do a good deed, it's very hard to keep it to ourselves. Part of that is because we often surprise ourselves. We let an elderly person go ahead of us at the supermarket, then mentally ask, "Wow, where did *that* come from?" Our reward may be a smile, or it may be nothing more than a warm internal feeling.

"Take heed that you do not do your charitable deeds before men, to be seen by them. Otherwise you have no reward from your Father in heaven."
MATTHEW 6:1 NKJV

Random acts of kindness are never planned and seldom rewarded by those around us at the time. They are secrets between two people and God. But God remembers them and they will be rewarded.

Father, we may or may not have the means to give generously to charity,
but we all have the ability to give of ourselves.
When we do, help us not to seek or expect the praise of others.
You see. That's enough.

Week 27

> All your children shall be
> taught by the LORD,
> and great shall be
> the peace of your children.
> ISAIAH 54:13 NKJV

We can prepare our children for life on their own, but the best thing we can do for them is to introduce them to the Lord. He is the only One who can give them peace.

What is the greatest hope you have for your children? Isn't it that, no matter what they become or accomplish, they should be happy? How can you teach them that? Your children may be rich or poor, famous or humble, but only God's peace will bring them true happiness.

Father, only You and Your lessons can give our children the happiness we want for them.
We do the best we can for them and trust the rest to You.

_____

_____

_____

_____

_____

_____

_____

_____

_____

_____

_____

_____

_____

_____

Almost everything we count on in life has the potential of failing us, of letting us down when we need
it the most. Love cools, trust is betrayed, hope is
lost. Parents can fail us, children can turn against
us, friends can become enemies. Eventually, even
our own bodies will betray us and fail to function
properly.

> For You are my hope,
> O Lord GOD;
> You are my trust from my youth.
> By You I have been
> upheld from my birth.
> PSALM 71:5–6 NKJV

Only God is eternal and never changing, the One who holds us
up and never betrays our trust. Only God gives us hope in our darkest moments when all
else has failed.

Lord, in a disappointing, human world,
You are our strength,
the One we turn to when we are alone and afraid.
Thank You for Your constant,
abiding love that brightens our lives.

This weekend look back and recall your most difficult times. Don't dwell on the people or things that failed you, but on the One who did not. How did God get you through the hard times? Did you recognize His help, or are you just beginning to appreciate His blessings now? Did He answer your prayers at the time or teach you how to survive through your own strength? Did He send you a helper when you needed one most, or did He make you a helper for someone else? Look at all the various ways He has been there for you and give Him the thanks He deserves.

"I am the ruler of this house, and we'll do it my way," he said.

"You are the king here," his wife admitted, "but do you know the difference between an absolute monarch and a constitutional one?"

Wives, submit unto your own husbands, as unto the Lord.
EPHESIANS 5:22 KJV

"Ah. . . ."

"An absolute monarch holds total authority. His wishes are supreme." She paused. "There aren't many of them around today."

"No?"

She shook her head. "A constitutional monarch rules with the consent of his or her subjects. They give the king his powers, and they can take them away. They can do away with the whole office or make him just a figurehead."

"I get it. I'm a constitutional monarch, but you hold all the real power."

"Yes, your highness," she replied with a smile.

Lord, no matter how we divide the responsibilities between us,
You are the absolute monarch of our family,
and we seek Your guidance in every matter.

For I am not ashamed of
the gospel of Christ.
ROMANS 1:16 KJV

What do you say when someone asks if you are a religious person? It may be a neighbor who sees you leaving for church every Sunday morning or a coworker who notices you pausing to whisper grace before a business lunch. Do you have the strength to answer their question with a simple yes? Or do you laugh it off with a "No, not really"?

Our response to that type of question will usually depend on the circumstances. Sometimes are not right for a detailed profession of faith, and some are. But at no time should we let others make us feel ashamed of our beliefs.

Father, some of us are tongue-tied in matters of faith,
while others are perfectly comfortable in such discussions.
You know our capabilities and weaknesses
and will help us never to be ashamed of our faith.

Accounts of natural disasters, be they floods, fires, earthquakes, or hurricanes, are splashed almost daily on front pages around the world. We feel powerless to protect ourselves on so many fronts, knowing the best we can do is react to disasters when they come, not prevent them.

> And they shall no more be a prey to the heathen, neither shall the beast of the land devour them; but they shall dwell safely, and none shall make them afraid.
> EZEKIEL **34:28** KJV

Yet God promises the righteous that they will dwell in safety, and even prosper in this dangerous world as a sign of His care and love. Above all, "none shall make them afraid."

Father, we thank You for Your protection in difficult times.
Although we may taste some suffering, You are our strength and Sustainer.

For if our heart condemns us,
God is greater than our heart,
and knoweth all things.
1 JOHN 3:20 KJV

We disappoint ourselves so easily. True, we are sinful beings, but we want to be better, and when we aren't we suffer the pangs of guilt. This is especially true in our relationships with our spouses, the ones we love so much and often treat so poorly.

At the end of a bad day, our husbands or wives bear the brunt of our disappointments and defeats. Why do they put up with us? Because they understand, they know our true hearts, and they love us in spite of ourselves.

Father, when we dump all our troubles on each other,
give our partners Your comfort.
Help us overcome our guilt for the sake of our love.

After a few years of marriage, we become so attuned to the other that we find ourselves completing each other's sentences. We anticipate what the other will want, bringing out a snack without being asked or folding the paper to highlight an article we know the other will want to read. We go so far as to turn down invitations we know the other would dread. In many little ways, the two of us have truly become one.

When you are feeling far away from God, remember that He knows and loves you even more than your spouse does. He anticipates your wants and needs, just as your spouse does, and always wants to please you.

And it shall come to pass, that before they call, I will answer; and while they are yet speaking, I will hear.
ISAIAH 65:24 KJV

Father, thank You for bringing us so close,
and remind us that this is just a taste of how You feel for us.

And even to your old age I am he;
and even to hoar hairs will I carry you:
I have made, and I will bear;
even I will carry, and will deliver you.
ISAIAH 46:4 KJV

Old age frightens us. What if we cannot care for ourselves or our spouse? Will we become a burden to our children? Will we outlive our savings? Who will love us when we turn into irritable old men and sharp-tongued old women?

God promises that He will care for us in our old age, even if others fail us. If necessary, He will pick us up and carry us, for He made us and loves us and will always take care of us.

*Father, thank You for this promise that gives us comfort as
our hair turns gray and our strength fades.
Getting old can be a burden, but You will always support us.*

This weekend think about your future and begin to draw up a plan that will provide for your old age. You may need the advice of a financial planner, so ask around for references and plan to make an appointment early in the week. What are others you know doing to provide financial security for their old age? The earlier you start, the less you will have to put aside every month to reach your goal.

Weeping may endure
for a night,
but joy cometh
in the morning.
PSALM 30:5 KJV

Relationships have their ups and downs. A thought-less comment, the wrong tone of voice, or even a look can wound us. But when tempers cool and reason returns, the disagreement usually proves to have been a waste of precious time and emotion.

The same thing happens in our relationship with God. We get angry with Him, and He probably gets angry with us, but we both are quick to forgive. It's hard to stay angry with someone who loves you totally, no matter how foolishly you act.

Father, Your forgiveness and the joy it brings us are examples of
the way we should treat our partners when we disagree or have our feelings hurt.
Remind us of that the next time we feel wounded by the other.

As we watch the news or read the newspaper, we may feel our blood pressure start to rise. Accounts of murderers, child molesters, terrorists, and others who hurt innocent people stir us into righteous indignation. We hope the law will deal as harshly with them as they did to others. And if they get away with it, we often wonder where God is.

For the wrath of man worketh not the righteousness of God.
JAMES 1:20 KJV

But God reminds us that our wrath has nothing to do with His righteousness. We could be wrong but He never is. While He will always understand our wrath, we cannot begin to understand His righteousness.

Father, we know You are there when the innocent suffer,
and we trust Your judgment of the evil ones in our midst.
Our justice may fail, but Yours will not.

The discretion of a man
deferreth his anger;
and it is his glory to
pass over a transgression.
PROVERBS 19:11 KJV

Some people are unflappable. They remain cool and composed when the rest of us would go into orbit. Are they totally emotionless, unable to love or hate? If you are married to such a person, the temptation is to try to pick a fight now and then, just to see if anything rattles your spouse.

Yet the Bible tells us that discreet people do have emotions and do get angry. Yet they "pass over" the transgressions of others, much as God does with ours, and this is to their glory. Trying to pick a fight with such people will not work. They will feel hurt and then they will forgive you—which will only drive you crazy.

Lord, we are two very different people who react differently to anger and pain.
Give us understanding and patience with each other.

Even the best Christians have days when God seems to be concentrating on the other side of the world. He certainly doesn't seem tuned in to our problems. We need help—right now, if you please—and we don't seem to be getting it. Where is God? Doesn't He love and care for us anymore?

The answer, of course, is that God is right there, just behind our shoulder, covering our backs and providing everything He promised to provide. He is always faithful, even when our emotions cause us to doubt that faithfulness.

If we believe not,
yet he abideth faithful.
2 TIMOTHY 2:13 KJV

Father, forgive our impatience and our doubts.
We are weak where You are strong,
imperfect where You are perfect.

Seest thou a man wise
in his own conceit?
there is more hope of a fool
than of him.
PROVERBS 26:12 KJV

We all know people who believe they know everything. A question comes up, they state the answer, and that's that. They don't even have to think about a problem to be right in their own eyes. In that lies their downfall, because a fool who takes time to think about a problem will come up with a better solution than someone who believes he has all the answers.

If you are married to one of these people, your patience will be sorely tested. You may have a wonderful, loving spouse, but sometimes you'll want to shake him or her and yell, "*Think* about it, will you?" Sometimes, because that person loves you, he or she will.

Lord, we know that only You are right all the time,
but we have too much faith in ourselves.
At such times, have patience with us and gently show us where
we are wrong so we may follow Your guidance in our lives.

Vanity reigns today, for both sexes. Plastic surgery can deal with almost any bodily "fault," and diets not only take care of unwanted pounds but promise a long and healthy life. If you'd look better as a blond, that can be arranged. If your thighs are out of control, hit the gym. Of course it's all vanity. In the end, you will still age. Your eyes will lose their focus, your muscles will ache, and your hair will fall out. You won't be able to stop any of it. Wouldn't all that time and effort be better spent working for the Lord?

Favour is deceitful,
and beauty is vain:
but a woman that feareth the LORD,
she shall be praised.
PROVERBS 31:30 KJV

Father, we know there is a difference between keeping fit and vanity. Help us find the proper balance in our lives and spend as much time helping others as we spend on ourselves.

Where do we draw the line between fitness and vanity? Each person has his or her own answer to that question. See if you can draw up a list illustrating where fitness ends and vanity begins. Is a nose job vanity, or is there a medical reason for considering it? Do you really believe that following the latest diet will help you live forever, or are you following your doctor's orders? How many inches do you want to work off your waistline, and is that a reasonable goal? Do you spend all your free time at the gym or play with your children? What are your priorities at this stage of your life? Would God approve of them?

_____

_____

_____

_____

_____

_____

_____

_____

_____

_____

_____

_____

_____

_____

_____

_____

_____

_____

Conversation reveals the inner person. When we're dating, we absorb every word our date utters and file each precious comment away for future reference. Some of our dates disqualify themselves the moment they open their mouths, but then we find the right one and marry, largely because of what that person said.

> Listen, for I have worthy things to say; I open my lips to speak what is right.
> PROVERBS 8:6 NIV

A few years later, we stop listening. We know our spouse so well that his or her comments are predictable and we've heard them all before. We stop talking about hopes and dreams and beliefs and limit our conversation to the weather, work, and children.

It doesn't have to be this way. Listen to your spouse with as much attention and affection as you listened while you were dating and you may find your love is deeper than you ever imagined.

*Lord, remind us of those long conversations we used to have
and how they helped our love to grow.
We still have much to learn about each other, if we will only listen.*

> For God is not
> a God of disorder
> but of peace.
> 1 CORINTHIANS 14:33 NIV

Life is not neat. It's full of disorder, loose ends, and unresolved conflicts that keep us from feeling at peace. There's no point at which we can clap our hands and say, "There! The children are grown. That part of our life is over."

In the same vein, we can never say, "We have overcome all our faults. We're perfect now," or "We have all we need saved up for retirement." As humans, we will never be free of disorder. God, however, brings order out of chaos. He knows how all our stories end and is happy to point out the way we should go.

The next time you are overwhelmed by life's disorder, place it all in God's hand and taste His peace.

Father, life can be so confusing when we rely on our own actions.
Help us turn our problems over to You,
the only source of true peace and order.

Have you ever been to an awards banquet and heard your spouse praised to the skies by people you don't even know? It doesn't take long before you wonder who these people are talking about.

> Jesus said to them, "Only in his hometown, among his relatives and in his own house is a prophet without honor."
> MARK 6:4 NIV

His successful planning lifted a company out of financial disaster? He can't even balance the family checkbook! Her insightful article brought positive public relations to the firm? They should see the inside of her medicine cabinet! Who *is* this person you live with?

It's hard to honor someone when you intimately know his or her every fault, but it's foolish to laugh when your spouse is praised by others. Smile proudly, accept their compliments at face value, and honor the one you love.

*Father, we don't know each other as well as we think,
and we seldom give each other deserved credit.
Make us proud of our spouses' achievements because they honor us, too.*

> Remember ye not
> the former things,
> neither consider
> the things of old.
>
> ISAIAH **43:18** KJV

We all go into marriage with twenty or thirty years of baggage, a good part of which is dirty laundry. We have a past, and not all of it was pretty. Most of this will come out during courtship, but not all.

While there will still be unconfessed episodes in every couple's past life, marriage is a new start, and no one should let the burdens of the past hang over the present. Confess what you can and forget the rest. God forgives your sins, so give them up and enjoy your new life as a couple.

Father, even when we confess our sins to You and receive Your forgiveness,
we may not be able to confess them to each other.
Don't let the past ruin our present.
Help us accept Your forgiveness and be at peace with our past.

When the kids are grown and gone, leaving the two of you to rattle around the house alone, you may make the astounding discovery that your best friend is your own spouse. You will still have other friends, but your best friend will be the one with whom you've shared most of a lifetime.

> Do not forsake your friend.
> PROVERBS 27:10 NIV

Such a discovery usually comes as a surprise. The passion of youth may have faded, and you've certainly had your share of arguments and disagreements, but the one you trust and love the most is still the same. What a joy to grow old with your best friend!

Father, thank You for all You have given us as a couple,
especially for the deep, abiding friendship we still share after all these years.

SATURDAY

> And Jacob loved Rachel;
> and said,
> I will serve thee seven years
> for Rachel thy younger daughter.
> GENESIS 29:18 KJV

Young people think it's romantic the way Jacob gave up seven years of his life for Rachel. Such sacrifice and devotion! They never stop to think that once the seven years were over, Jacob signed up for a lifetime of service to Rachel, binding himself to love her, protect her, and help her raise the children. Compared to that, the seven years were a snap.

Romance is wonderful, but reality is even more so. The next time you feel that love has grown cold in your marriage, remember all the daily sacrifices your spouse has made for the sake of the family. Hanging in there for all those years is far more romantic than seven years of waiting.

Lord, remind us that true love is shown in the daily business of living.
It may not be romantic, but it brings us together
and shows us exactly what You mean love to be: service to others.

This weekend why not let your spouse know how much you appreciate him or her? Think back and recall all the sacrifices made for your family, all the diapers your husband changed, all the meals your wife provided. What do you appreciate most in each other? What do you still need from your spouse? What will you need in the future?

> A man who lacks judgment
> derides his neighbor,
> but a man of understanding
> holds his tongue.
> PROVERBS 11:12 NIV

Couples usually see more of their neighbors than they do their relatives. That's good, as neighbors are likely to be more helpful than relatives in a crisis, simply because they're closer. You might not choose your neighbors as friends—you sort of work with what you have—but you do have much in common with them and would do well to keep neighborly relations polite and friendly.

One of the best ways of doing this is to never say a bad word about one neighbor to another, no matter what the provocation. Your words will always come back to haunt you. The best advice is still to love your neighbor.

Lord, remind us to treat all our neighbors with respect and use discretion in our conversations with them.

People are becoming polarized by food. Many, indeed, are almost militant about what they and others should or should not eat. A strict vegetarian might look at you and your steak and react as though you had committed murder. A dedicated meat eater might consider a vegetarian a wimp. Some people eat whatever is put in front of them, while others make a big deal out of a meal they can't eat.

But there's no sense in bringing such disagreements to the table, especially if you are a guest. Meals should be a time of love and sharing, not a scene of conflict between different food philosophies.

> Better a meal of vegetables where there is love than a fattened calf with hatred.
> PROVERBS 15:17 NIV

Father, help us be sensitive to the beliefs of others when we entertain and not be argumentative when we are someone's guest.

> Splendor and majesty
> are before Him,
> strength and beauty
> are in His sanctuary.
> PSALM 96:6 NASB

You may think of your wife as beautiful, but you probably don't often ponder God's beauty.

None of us know what Jesus looked like on earth, yet He wasn't physically attractive (see Isaiah 53:2). Still, the Psalmist isn't talking about God's face; he's commenting on His personality.

Perhaps you've known someone who wouldn't win a beauty contest but had a "great personality." After a while, you didn't care what that person looked like—you were friends. God is something like that. Once you know Him, though you can't see His face, you know His beauty and want more of Him.

God isn't just a pretty personality. He also has unlimited splendor, majesty, and strength. The more you look at Him, the more there is to see.

Have you looked at Him today and seen His strength? Have you seen His splendor and worshiped His majesty?

Come close to Him today.

Father God, we don't often appreciate Your beauty, strength, splendor, and majesty.
Forgive us for our shallowness. We want to know You better.

Telling the truth takes courage. People don't like to hear the truth when they're caught up in pleasant but disastrous lies. They'd rather enjoy the fun now and ignore the price they'll pay down the road.

Telling the truth in marriage can be particularly hard. After all, you can't stage a "truth attack" and then walk away. You have to live with your spouse day in and day out.

> "And like their bow
> they have bent their tongues for lies.
> They are not valiant for
> the truth on the earth.
> For they proceed from evil to evil,
> and they do not know Me,"
> says the LORD.
> JEREMIAH 9:3 NKJV

We all need to understand that ignoring the truth just gets us into deeper trouble. In biblical terms, we go "from evil to evil." Avoiding evil means listening to a truthful spouse, weighing his or her words, and being willing to make changes.

Truth isn't our enemy, and neither is that spouse. A reality check that draws us closer to God may be a spouse's loving gift.

Lord, teach us to speak gentle truth to each other and to know when it has been spoken.

> Your father, the devil
> . . . was a murderer from the beginning,
> not holding to the truth,
> for there is no truth in him.
> When he lies,
> he speaks his native language,
> for he is a liar and the father of lies.
>
> JOHN 8:44 NIV

The "father of lies," Satan, has fooled many people into believing that marriage is a partnership of misery. Out of fear they shun it, living together instead or completely avoiding relationships.

Satan's lie murders marriage. But how can people whose parents fought and made each other unhappy understand marital happiness? How can they believe in something they've never seen?

Happily married Christians kill Satan's lie by making their marriages witnesses to young people caught in doubt. By sharing time with others, telling them of God's plan for marriage, letting them see marital joy, and providing an example of positive behavior, Christians shine light into lives darkened by Satan's lies.

God's truth begins in the home, with our own families, and beams out into the world.

Lord, we offer our marriage up to You,
as a witness to the truth of Your love.
We want to show forth the truth of the life You have established.

_____

_____

_____

_____

_____

_____

_____

_____

_____

You've heard all the public promises about the goodness of life. "All is fine," politicians say. "You don't have to worry!" But suddenly a disaster strikes, and the emptiness of those words becomes apparent.

> For when they shall say,
> Peace and safety:
> then sudden destruction
> cometh upon them,
> as travail upon a woman with child;
> and they shall not escape.
> 1 THESSALONIANS 5:3 KJV

Spiritually a day is coming when the emptiness of unfulfilled promises to God will be shown. People who claimed to know Jesus, but don't, will be shocked to discover the everlasting life they could have had, had they made a lasting commitment. Those folks may be family members, friends—or even us.

No one should be fooled by words of safety. None of us can escape spiritually if we are trying to "butter up" God, though our hearts are cold toward Him.

Only in our commitment to Him are we truly safe, and our hearts are the thermometers that show our spiritual temperatures.

How many degrees is your heart registering now?

Whether we're speaking to friends or family, Lord,
people need to hear Your offer of love.
Fire up our hearts today.

How can you make your marriage a Christian testimony? First take a look at your own relationship. Is it happy? Do you need to work on many spots, or can you honestly say your marriage, while not perfect, can witness to God's love?

If your marriage needs strengthening, perhaps you need an example. Discover couples with strong marriages in your church or family and see if you can get some good advice from them. Discuss with such a couple what they think has worked for them and what they think has contributed to their success.

If you have a strong marriage, how can you help others? Consider ways you can become a testimony by "showing forth your light" to those who are doubtful about marriage or need to do some marital fine-tuning. You don't need a degree in counseling to listen to others and share solutions that have worked for you, but be sure you meet together as a couple or with the mate of your sex. Counseling the opposite sex can put your own marriage at risk.

How can you increase your love for other Christians? Paul doesn't offer "The Twelve Steps of Brotherly Love" or give the Thessalonians any new directions on how to love each other. That lesson comes directly from God.

> But as touching brotherly love ye need not that I write unto you: for ye yourselves are taught of God to love one another.
>
> 1 THESSALONIANS 4:9 KJV

When it comes to our brothers and sisters in Christ, God shows us ways to love them. We hear of a need here and fill it. We become aggravated at a brother's actions and deal with them gently or let them pass, as God guides us. The Spirit works in our hearts to show what is best.

Only when we ignore His still, small voice do we land ourselves in trouble. Without His guidance, small problems increase and destroy a church. Little sins, constantly fed, become large problems.

Whether that "brother" is your spouse or a Christian from your congregation, listen to God's voice. A few quiet moments with God are worth a thousand steps.

Thank You, Lord, for showing us how to love one another.
This day, fill our hearts with ways to express that love.

> We are bound to thank God
> always for you, brethren. . .
> because that your faith groweth exceedingly, and
> the charity of every one of you
> all toward each other aboundeth.
> 2 THESSALONIANS 1:3 KJV

Though they faced great pressure, the Thessalonians had one thing down pat: They knew how to love each other. Persecution and trials hadn't made these Christians turn on each other. If anything, such torments had purified their love.

When we face trials, how do we act? Do we turn to each other for support or head off in opposite directions, saying, "It's all my spouse's fault"?

None of us need to experience a faith persecution to find how we'd respond. We discover our mettle when money becomes tight or a family member is in trouble. Suddenly it can become "my money" versus "your money" or "my family" opposing "yours."

The Thessalonians pleased God—and Paul—by feeding their faith, not dissension. And in the end they blessed themselves by sharing a greater brotherly love. Are you blessing yourselves, too?

We need to love each other and fellow Christians, Lord.
Open our hearts to the words of Your Spirit.

It almost goes without saying that not everyone you meet in life will be a Christian. A few non-believers will get your goat, drive you nuts, and make you wish you'd never met them. They'll make unreasonable demands or do downright evil things. Perhaps they'll even demand that you act as if you didn't have any faith. Certainly, they don't welcome your witness.

> Finally, brethren, pray for us. . . that we may be delivered from unreasonable and wicked men: for all men have not faith. But the Lord is faithful.
> 2 THESSALONIANS 3:1–3 KJV

Just because God graced Paul with an amazing set of spiritual gifts didn't keep Paul from running into guys who stood in the way of the spread of the Gospel. Paul doesn't sound as if he relished knowing these folks.

Like Paul, we meet people who accept our testimony about God and those who cause us nothing but grief. We thank Him for our "Thessalonians," who eagerly hear more, and we sometimes pray for deliverance from the others.

But whether we thank or pray, we trust in God's faithfulness. After all, that's what spreads the Gospel in the end.

When we run into people who don't like our message, Lord,
help us remember that it's Yours, not ours.

> But ye, brethren,
> be not weary in well doing.
> 2 THESSALONIANS 3:13 KJV

About time someone told the brethren that, some woman out there is thinking. Women often tend to do a lot of "well doing." Caring for families, taking part in church activities, and facing an overloaded "to-do" list can make them irritable. After all, how can anyone fit one more task on that mile-long sheet?

But God isn't just speaking to men here; He's talking to all Christians. "Well doing" doesn't mean having the longest to-do list or being on every church board. It means not giving up on doing right: loving that child who is straying, responding to hatred with love, and hanging in there when times are tough.

There will be times when doing right doesn't seem to get its proper payback or when the difficult situation seems stronger than we are. "Do not get weary," Paul says. God will give you strength.

All of us need His strength for just one more day, and one more hour, to hold on all the way.

Give us Your strength, gracious Lord, when we feel tempted to give in.
We need Your energy, flowing through us, to complete Your tasks.

—————————————————————————————
—————————————————————————————
—————————————————————————————
—————————————————————————————
—————————————————————————————
—————————————————————————————
—————————————————————————————
—————————————————————————————
—————————————————————————————
—————————————————————————————
—————————————————————————————
—————————————————————————————

"*Lazybones* should not be another name for 'Christian,'" Paul might have said. Concerned about believers who seemed to think awaiting the Second Coming of Christ was a great opportunity to loaf, the apostle feared these idle folk could ruin the witness of the entire body (see 1 Thessalonians 4:11–12).

> For even when we were with you, this we commanded you, that if any would not work, neither should he eat.
> 2 THESSALONIANS 3:10 KJV

Paul wasn't trying to starve needy people; he was just trying to keep believers from being so heavenly minded that they were no earthly good. Earthly needs were still part of the Christians' lives. It was not right to have healthy, able people milking the hard workers in the congregation.

Caring for others means you don't let them fall into bad habits without laying down the law. You don't encourage sin simply because you fear conflict.

Confronting with love isn't easy but it may be necessary.

*Lord, we know You could return any day.
We want to be diligent in serving You every day.*

> "When you see the ark
> of the covenant of
> the Lord your God,
> and the priests, who are Levites, carrying it,
> you are to move out from
> your positions and follow it.
> Then you will know which way to go,
> since you have never been
> this way before."
>
> JOSHUA 3:3–4 NIV

Wouldn't it be great to just look up and see where God is leading you? Lift your eyes and God's ark would show you the way. The Israelites could hardly make a mistake, with God so obviously present.

For a short time, all *was* well. The Israelites crossed the Jordan. But in Joshua 7:7 their leader started questioning why God brought them into the Promised Land. "Are you going to destroy us?" Joshua asked. Discouragement, caused by sin, had obliterated that obvious path.

God doesn't usually lead by putting a physical sign before us. He leads our hearts. When we don't open them to His way, He could drive a Mack truck before us, and we wouldn't see it.

Are your hearts open to Him today?

Lord, we don't need an ark in front of us to see Your will.
Open our hearts so we can follow Your path.

Loving "the brethren" may seem simple, but how about loving your brothers and sisters? Now that can be a challenge.

This week get in touch with at least one of your siblings. Spend time together, if you can, or if distance is a problem, write a note, e-mail, or make a phone call.

If troublesome issues part you, pray before you speak to your sibling or choose to write a letter that might help you reconcile. Perhaps the best you can do is to let your sibling know that you care, even if you can't agree.

Should a sibling be totally out of touch, pray for that person. When you cannot reach out, God can.

Don't have any siblings you can reach out to? Try another relative or a friend you've lost touch with lately.

> And Joshua said,
> "Ah, Sovereign LORD,
> why did you ever bring this people
> across the Jordan to deliver us into the
> hands of the Amorites to destroy us?
> If only we had been content to stay
> on the other side of the Jordan!"
> JOSHUA 7:7 NIV

Sovereign Lord? The words that follow seem to show that Joshua missed the point entirely. If God is sovereign and can do what He wills, the leader of the Hebrews could trust that God had a purpose for bringing them across the Jordan. A sovereign God was still in control, and Joshua could trust in Him.

We know what it's like to struggle as Joshua did. We start on a path, certain of God's direction. At first, all is clear and life runs smoothly. Then we hit the first roadblock. "Ah, Sovereign Lord," we cry, "how did we get ourselves in this mess?"

The ark isn't out in front of us anymore. We have to trust, and that isn't always easy. But we, too, can look back at the "Jordans" God has carried us across, the sins He's wiped out of our lives and the situations He's brought us through.

No matter what we face, He still is sovereign Lord.

Lord, when it's hard to trust in You,
remind us that You are sovereign Lord.
Reign over our lives.

_____

_____

_____

_____

_____

_____

_____

_____

_____

_____

_____

_____

_____

"See, Joshua, I didn't plan to wipe you out," God might have said. "All that worrying for nothing."

Israel won the battle of Ai the second time, when they followed God's will. The sin of one man, Achan, had lost them the first battle, and that sin had to be uncovered and dealt with before Israel could move on. God had given His people a graphic demonstration that sin kills.

> For when Joshua and all Israel saw that the ambush had taken the city and that smoke was going up from the city, they turned around and attacked the men of Ai.
>
> JOSHUA 8:21 NIV

But obedience brings the believer victory, even over those places where struggle has gone before. Sin may block success for a season, but obedience defeats sin's rule in our lives.

Is there an Ai in your lives? Seek out sin and replace it with obedience. God will help you triumph.

Forgive us, Lord, for those things we have done or omitted to do.
Show us where we must obey to show forth Your triumph.

> Now faith is
> the assurance of things hoped for,
> the conviction of things not seen.
> HEBREWS 11:1 NASB

Faith is for those moments when nothing seems to go right. When you've reached the end of your rope and just can't hold on, and you wish you could live someone else's life—one with no troubles—you need faith.

That's because faith is tied to hope. One doesn't come without the other. When you're stuck in a tough situation, you need to be able to hold on to hope and to see the unseen long enough to know that your situation is not forever.

The author of Hebrews continues by listing many men and women and the benefits of their faith. They didn't physically receive all God's promises any more than we do, but they held on in faith, receiving many benefits in this life and an eternal reward.

When life isn't going perfectly, hold on to your convictions and someday you'll be glorifying God, along with Abel, Enoch, Noah, Abraham, Sarah. . . .

Following so great a cloud of witnesses who trusted in You,
we need not doubt, O Lord.

_____

_____

_____

_____

_____

_____

_____

_____

_____

_____

_____

Okay, your faith isn't perfect. There *are* days when doubt and trouble get you down. Abraham and Sarah had them, too. But they kept their eyes in the right place and those imperfect days didn't destroy them.

> Therefore, since we have so great a cloud of witnesses surrounding us, let us lay aside every encumbrance. . . fixing our eyes on Jesus, the author and perfecter of faith.
> HEBREWS 12:1–2 NASB

We don't perfect our faith. It's not a matter of getting every spiritual jot and tittle right and making a daily exhibition of massive self-control. If we micromanaged our lives like that, we'd never become perfect. We'd end up being legalistic instead.

But when we focus on Jesus, changes happen in our lives. While we're not even looking—because we have our eyes on Him—we start experiencing an unexpected fruit of the Spirit. We were obeying Him in one place, and He gave us an unanticipated gift.

We're just focusing on the Master, along with that great cloud of witnesses who have gone before us.

We want to keep our eyes on You, Lord.
Keep our vision fixed there.

> For whatsoever is born of God
> overcometh the world:
> and this is the victory that
> overcometh the world,
> even our faith.
> Who is he that overcometh the world,
> but he that believeth that Jesus is
> the Son of God?
> 1 JOHN 5:4–5 KJV

Overcoming sounds hard, doesn't it? Climbing a mountain or fighting off an enemy might make an appropriate word picture, but faith in Jesus? That somehow seems too simple. Faith seems too lightweight a concept to overcome anything.

But our mistaken preconceptions won't do here. John isn't talking about a touchy-feely faith that's strong one day and weak the next. He's talking about the Christian who takes risks for his faith or suffers for her beliefs.

Overcoming the world isn't a piece of cake. It takes great effort to do the right thing when wrong is so tempting. Doing God's will, when the world says it's silly, challenges us.

Those struggles we go through aren't meaningless, though they may seem so at the time. They're really indicators of overcoming.

Are both of you overcoming today?

Lord, when we face struggles,
help us to see them as indicators that we're overcoming the world—for You.

When faith seems difficult, we struggle to understand its privileges. Trials conceal the truth concerning the benefits that come with being God's child.

Unbelief obscures the tender care He has for His children. After all, nonbelievers would find it hard to believe that God cared much for their greatest problems, much less the intimate details of their day. Only with faith comes the certainty of love.

As God's children, you can be confident He cares for every trouble, even the small, irritating ones that still ruin a day in seconds.

Face the loss of a loved one or a minor argument with the same confidence: God cares for your troubles. Cry out softly or shout it from the rooftops, and He will hear.

> The righteous cry out,
> and the Lord hears them;
> he delivers them from
> all their troubles.
> PSALM 34:17 NIV

Lord, You have shown Your love in so many ways,
yet we still miss the point.
Thank You for the privilege of coming to You with even our small irritations.

Faith can be hard work—or it can seem like a simple slide into God's kingdom. How you feel about it today probably depends on your situation right now.

But faith is not a matter of feelings. Faith is based on something much stronger: God.

To discover more about faith, use a concordance to look up words like *faith, faithful, sovereign, obey,* and *trust.* (If there is no concordance in the back of your Bible, or you don't have a separate one, stop by a Christian bookstore and pick one up. A concordance is an essential tool for Bible study.) Read the verses together and discuss what you learn about faith. How can it impact your lives?

Most Christians don't feel comfortable boasting.
Advertising our own qualities isn't very humble,
and we surely wouldn't think of standing up in
church and tooting our own horns.

> My soul will boast in the Lord;
> let the afflicted hear and rejoice.
> PSALM 34:2 NIV

No one wants to listen to that kind of self-praise any-
way. Praising friends and family is better, but even that can get old fast.

But boasting about God is another matter. We can't say anything good about Him and
be off the mark. We can't make a wonderful declaration and lie about Him. He outdoes all
our expectations. Though people might tire of boasts about humans, those who love God
never dislike hearing about His good deeds.

If we praise God—in our homes, at church, or in the marketplace—we may run into
people who don't like it. But we'll also bless hurting people. Hearing about Jesus can lift
the saddest heart, when it's tuned in to His praise.

Though we cannot boast in our own accomplishments,
we can always say something great about You, O Lord.
May our mouths always sing Your praises.

> So he gave them his attention,
> expecting to receive
> something from them.
> Then Peter said,
> "...What I do have I give you:
> In the name of Jesus Christ of Nazareth,
> rise up and walk."
> ACTS 3:5–6 NKJV

That morning when the lame man came to the gate, perhaps he'd mumbled a prayer for help, but doubtless he hadn't expected much of an answer. A few coins were all he wanted. Not much to ask for, was it, God? After all everyone has to live.

Hope didn't have a chance in his heart. Two men who didn't have a penny on them approached. One spoke, and the beggar no longer needed to beg. Where once hope had died, it rose expectantly.

Feeling hopeless today? Jesus still makes life changes in people who don't expect them. He comes to those who are far from Him and calls their names. Suddenly, like the lame man, they're whole and hopeful.

Have you turned to the One who heals beggars? All you have to do is ask.

Lord, our expectations are often so much smaller than Yours.
Light hope in our hearts.

_____

_____

_____

_____

_____

_____

_____

_____

_____

_____

_____

_____

People of David's day could have asked him, "What makes your God better than ours? How come *ours* are the idols?" Pagans believed gods ruled over certain territories. So Yahweh having control over Israel was no problem, as long as He didn't try to control the Canaanites' or the Egyptians' lands, which had their own deities.

> For all the gods of the peoples are idols, but the LORD made the heavens.
> 1 CHRONICLES 16:26 NKJV

If those doubting pagans lived today, they'd find their gods only in the history books. Maybe they'd start wondering, *Could those old Israelite prophets have been right anyway? Wouldn't the God who was real still be around after all these years?*

People today show the same attitude when they want you to accept all religions as being equal. They think all faiths get you to the same place and they condemn Christians as snobs.

But thousands of years from now, who will be worshiping their gods of money and "tolerance"? And who will be rejoicing in the One who made those heavens?

Lord Jesus, Son of the Living God,
You reach back through the ages and forward through eternity.
No idol vanquishes You.

A friend loves at all times,
and a brother is born
for adversity.
PROVERBS 17:17 NKJV

"Marry your best friend" is not bad advice, but that best friend you marry is still different from you. You do dishes right after supper, when he isn't ready. He does things at lightning speed, when you prefer a slower pace.

Minor marital differences can work for or against you, depending on how you deal with them. Turn each one into a fight and your relationship becomes a battleground. Recognize them for what they are—differences that aren't the end of the world—and peace reigns again.

Small issues that act like sand in the gears of your marriage don't have to ruin your relationship. God never said two people had to agree constantly, but they do have to love at all times and stick with each other through the trials. After all, if your spouse is a Christian, you married a brother or sister in the faith.

Treat your spouse with constant love, and you'll develop a great friendship—and a terrific romance.

Thank You, Lord, for the friendship You've given us.
Help us not to let the sand get in the gears of our marriage.

_____

_____

_____

_____

_____

_____

_____

_____

_____

_____

_____

One day life can seem good. Things are going your way and God seems to be "on your side." The next day disaster strikes and you're left looking miserable, while those awful sinners across the street or across town have a picture-perfect life.

> "Even if Babylon reaches the sky and fortifies her lofty stronghold, I will send destroyers against her," declares the LORD.
> JEREMIAH 51:53 NIV

"Why me, Lord?" you may cry. "Didn't I try to obey You? What went wrong?" You may be tempted to look at Mr. and Mrs. Sinner with a jaundiced eye and wonder why they aren't in your shoes instead.

You don't need to begin evening up the "score." God still has everything under control, both in your life and your neighbor's. Those who ignore God may have a reprieve during this lifetime—or they may have a world of silent misery inside—but God deals with them in His own time. It's not ours to judge and condemn.

When our trials come, whys or bitterness bring us nothing. Trusting that God is in control holds the real answer.

We may never know why,
but we know the One who holds "Why?" in His hands—You.

> Where then does
> wisdom come from?
> Where does understanding dwell?
> . . .God understands the way to it
> and he alone knows where it dwells.
> JOB 28:20, 23 NIV

Facing a tough decision? You probably feel you could use some wisdom. But where do you turn for really good information, for an unbiased view?

Look to anything on this earth and you are likely to meet with disappointment. Only God knows the answers you're seeking.

Those answers aren't hidden away in the deepest part of heaven. God shares His wisdom with His people so they can please Him. Like a father who wants to be proud of his children, the Almighty teaches His children how to live.

God isn't trying to keep information from you. His answers are found in His Word, through prayer, and in the counsel of those who walk close to Him.

If you don't have an answer yet, maybe He's clearly telling you to wait. You just don't want to hear that yet.

Lord, thank You for sharing Your infinite wisdom with us.
Open our hearts and minds to hear what You say.

Having faith often isn't a simple matter. Ideas that seem so easy in God's Word get tough when they meet a sinful world.

Hope and trust come hard to us when our lives are turned upside-down with trials or questions we can't answer. But the truth doesn't change, because we hope and trust in the One who created heaven and earth—and our own, sometimes-miserable lives.

Are you facing a challenge today? Whether it's a financial problem, a decision you have a hard time agreeing on, or a communication gap that threatens your marriage, God has an answer for you.

Begin by turning to His Word. If you know verses that can help you, turn to them together and share them. If you don't know where to look, open a concordance and look for key words about your troubles. Then read the verses together, writing down those that speak most clearly to your situation. Be sure to read the text around those verses, making sure you know what God is really saying.

End by discussing your situation and praying together. Thank God for His guidance, even if your way is not entirely clear.

> I will maintain
> my righteousness and
> never let go of it;
> my conscience will not reproach me
> as long as I live.
> JOB 27:6 NIV

Job's one admirable man! No matter what else happens, he will not lie. Though his "friends" criticize, he will not cave in to pressure and say, "Okay, I was wrong," just to get those pests off his back.

Sometimes well-meaning family and friends pressure us to do wrong. "It would be easier to do what your boss wants. Who cares if it isn't strictly honest?" Or, "What's the big deal if this nice pair of shoes fell off the back of a truck? Someone has to wear them. It might as well be you!" We may give in, thinking, *Why make them unhappy, when it's such a tiny matter?*

Job wasn't getting a promotion or nice clothes. But he still wouldn't lie over a "small" thing. After all, the holiness of the Lord of the universe wasn't small and Job wanted to be just like Him.

Lord, we want to be just like You.
Show us how not to cave in on the small stuff.

Need help? Ask your wife or husband—unless you're King Ahab, that is. Help like Jezebel's a spouse doesn't need.

> Jezebel his wife said, "Is this how you act as king over Israel? Get up and eat! Cheer up. I'll get you the vineyard of Naboth the Jezreelite."
> 1 KINGS 21:7 NIV

When Ahab wanted a vineyard and Naboth wouldn't sell his property, which was his inheritance, the king went home to sulk. But the king's wife, that tough cookie Jezebel, had a plan to fix everything: Kill Naboth, and take his land for yourself.

The tough cookies of this world often have it tough. They try harder and harder to make life go where they want, and things never seem to work out. That's because they're looking for vineyards when they should be looking to God. They're hoping this world will come up with answers that belong to the Almighty.

Want to help your spouse? Don't be a tough cookie—turn to God instead.

Lord, when we need help, we know where to go for it.
You have every answer to our needs. We turn to You today.

> Now the people complained
> about their hardships in
> the hearing of the LORD,
> and when he heard them
> his anger was aroused.
> NUMBERS 11:1 NIV

Complaints quickly get hard to take. Mention something once and your spouse probably won't mind. Perhaps a second time will be okay, too, but once or twice more, and you'll end up with a marital squabble.

God didn't appreciate complaints from His people either. "Traveling all this way in the desert is a pain," some probably said. "It makes our feet sore." "We don't like the food!" objected others. Dissatisfaction rang in His ears, instead of the praises that should have been there. The Holy One became angry.

The complaints of His people showed they didn't really appreciate Him and His salvation from Egypt. He'd tried to lead them into the Promised Land but they'd objected. That sin of disobedience had landed them in the desert.

Don't turn your marriage into a desert of complaints. Instead, appreciate your spouse. You'll diffuse anger—and avoid sore feet!

We know we need to keep our complaints to a minimum, Lord.
Show us instead how to appreciate You and that special spouse.

_____

_____

_____

_____

_____

_____

_____

_____

_____

_____

_____

_____

_____

When David passed judgment on the wealthy man whom he thought had stolen another's only lamb, death seemed a just punishment. The king didn't know that the prophet who told him the tale was pointing out the monarch's own sin. David had stolen the only wife of Uriah the Hittite, committing adultery with her, and Nathan rebuked him through that story.

> David burned with anger against the man and said to Nathan, "As surely as the LORD lives, the man who did this deserves to die!"
> 2 SAMUEL 12:5 NIV

Until then, David thought he'd sinned without being caught. Thinking no one except he and Bathsheba knew, David forgot about God or thought He'd ignored that trespass.

We, too, think we "get away" with sin. God doesn't press us about a wrongdoing, so we think it's okay. But suddenly we find we've underestimated Him. What we've swept under the carpet trips us up again.

In your marriage are you tripping over sins? Bring them to God so He can sweep the bad out of your lives.

Sweep sin out of our lives, Lord God. We don't want anything to keep us from loving You.

"Why did you despise the word of the LORD by doing what is evil in his eyes?'"

2 SAMUEL 12:9 NIV

Have you ever despised the Word of the Lord?

We wouldn't do that, you may think. *A hallmark of believing Christians is love for God's Word: We love what God says because we love Him and want to obey Him.*

But if we really love God, we not only revere His Word, we obey it. When He declares something is wrong, we don't figure we'll do it "just this once." Sin doesn't slip into our lives as it did into David's.

We also don't want to use God's Word without compassion. For some, Scripture becomes a weapon to wound other believers who don't accept their legalistic interpretation. Their harsh adherence to man-made rules is not of God.

Take the Word seriously. God does. When Christians ignore or misuse it, He takes it very personally. Despise His Word, and you despise the One who gave it to you.

Lord, we love You and Your Word. Help us to obey You today.

_____

_____

_____

_____

_____

_____

_____

_____

_____

_____

_____

_____

_____

_____

_____

It's so hard to get up and going when rain is drumming on the roof and racing through the downspouts. You just want to pull the covers up over your shoulders and go back to sleep. But eventually your mind comes awake with an unpleasant jerk: You have twenty people arriving for a cookout this afternoon! Now what? Do you try to move the party to Sunday or Monday or pack them all into the house? There isn't much biblical advice on this modern problem, but life-giving rain is, in itself, a reason for celebration. Maybe you should just lie there and enjoy it for a while longer.

> And Elijah said unto Ahab, Get thee up, eat and drink; for there is a sound of abundance of rain.
> 1 KINGS 18:41 KJV

Father, when the weather messes up our plans,
help us remember that Your plans come first and that what may be
an inconvenience to some is often a blessing to others.

_____ SUNDAY _____

This weekend marks the end of summer, no matter what the calendar says. It's a time for cooking outside with friends we will see less of in the next few months, a time to buy school clothing for children who have shot up an inch or two over the long days of summer—a transition time when baseball is winding down and football is cranking up. Gather friends and family together, take a final dip in the pool, and burn some hot dogs in celebration.

This is a verse your children will heartily agree with, now that the freedom of summer is over and school looms ahead. Most of them are bored to death by now and secretly looking forward to school's opening, but not many will admit those feelings. They feel the way you do after a long family vacation: "That was fun, but it will be good to get back to normal life."

Of making many books there is no end, and much study is wearisome to the flesh.
ECCLESIASTES 12:12 NKJV

The next few weeks will be a time of adjustment for the whole family. Children will be exhausted and cranky when they get home, while parents will be faced with back-to-school meetings, teachers' conferences, and child-care adjustments. Be patient. Things will soon settle into a comfortable rut.

Father, help us all adjust to this new school year,
with its demands on our time and energy.
It's wonderful to see our children learn,
but it's a challenge to us all.

> For in much wisdom
> is much grief,
> and he who increases
> knowledge increases sorrow.
> ECCLESIASTES 1:18 NKJV

There's so much in the world that we wish we didn't know, so much that we hope our children will never learn through sad experience. War and famine come right into our living rooms after dinner with the early news, and the eleven o'clock news is hardly a source of pleasant dreams.

Yes, knowledge can bring us grief and sorrow. On the other hand, it also brings us awareness, compassion, and a sense of accountability. We are not alone in this world, and what we do here affects the lives of others on the opposite side of the earth.

Father, even when knowledge brings us sadness or anger,
we can turn these unpleasant emotions into good,
with Your help and guidance.
Show us what we need to do and how we can help repair the lives of others.

Being fallible, self-centered people, we usually look for ways to blame someone else when our lives go wrong. Ultimately, we are even tempted to wonder if something is wrong with God. Can't He hear our prayers? Is He too far away to pluck us from danger?

> Behold, the LORD's hand is not shortened, that it cannot save; neither his ear heavy, that it cannot hear.
> ISAIAH 59:1 KJV

The answer, of course, is that God is still—and will forever be—the same. He doesn't change, He hears fine, and He has all the power He needs. The problem is with us, not Him. We do God a grave injustice when we try to shift the blame to Him, instead of taking responsibility for our own lives.

Father, forgive us when we try to unburden our own shoulders and put the blame on You.

> So the women sang
> as they danced, and said:
> "Saul has slain his thousands,
> and David his ten thousands."
> 1 SAMUEL 18:7 NKJV

As soon as that highly public song of praise was sung, David was in deep trouble with Saul. Nothing he would ever do for Saul would take away the king's pain. Certainly Saul was emotionally unstable, but that song sent him over the edge.

We, too, have to be careful with our praise. If you have children, you want to praise their good actions but do it in such a way that your other children will not resent the "good" one. If you praise a fellow worker, are you doing it at the expense of another? Think before you sing that song of praise. Don't let it hurt anyone.

*Father, help us be fair in our praise and always mindful of
how it will affect others we love.*

_____

_____

_____

_____

_____

_____

_____

_____

_____

_____

_____

_____

_____

_____

"And the Lord turned and looked at Peter." What did Peter see in that brief glance from his doomed Savior? Disappointment? Anger? Probably not, although both would have been justified.

> And the Lord turned and looked at Peter. . . . Then Peter went out and wept bitterly.
> LUKE 22:61–62 NKJV

No, Peter saw nothing but love in that glance, which is why he ran out and wept so bitterly. He had promised undying love and then he had denied his Lord. Worse yet, the Lord still loved him, unworthy as he was.

The next time you and your spouse disagree, remember the Lord's reaction to disappointment. Stun your spouse with love.

Father, help us react to betrayal with love,
following Jesus' example in our own lives.

Let another man praise thee,
and not thine own mouth;
a stranger,
and not thine own lips.
PROVERBS 27:2 KJV

We all know people who can turn any subject into self-praise, no matter how remote the connection. You may be discussing a new book, only to have this person tell you he was reading at the age of two or once stopped for gas in the author's hometown. The logical reply to this is "So what?" but you're too polite to say that.

These people always need to be the center of attention, no matter what the subject. That they're committing conversational suicide never occurs to them. Pity them and hope they'll lose interest and wander away.

Father, we all do a little self-promotion now and then.
Make us aware whenever we cross the line and become a bore,
because self-praise is no praise at all.

While self-praise can be foolish and annoying, always putting yourself down is just as fool-ish. You do have good traits and talents, after all, and being a healthy person involves being aware of your strengths (but not boasting about them). This weekend take a merciful look at yourself. What do you do well? What talents do you have? Are you a better-than-average cook? A careful shopper? Can you always get the chain back on a child's bicycle? Can you tell when your spouse has had a bad day at work and help him or her forget about it? Can you set up a VCR in under ten minutes? Don't share this list with your spouse. This is just for you.

For this reason a man will leave
his father and mother
and be united to his wife,
and they will become one flesh.
GENESIS 2:24 NIV

The idea that one plus one equals one is hard for us to grasp, but that's what happens in marriage. A man and a woman come to the marriage ceremony as two separate individuals; when they walk back up the aisle, they are one couple. They both still maintain their individuality—nothing is taken away from either of them—yet now they are "Mr. and Mrs.," a new shared identity.

In a way, attending a wedding is similar to celebrating a birth, which is why the recessional of the new couple is often heartily applauded. Where once there were two, now there is one, and life goes on.

Father, help us both as we begin our new life as one.
We have much to learn and experience in this new state of marriage
but know You are there for us, celebrating with us.

_____
_____
_____
_____
_____
_____
_____
_____
_____
_____
_____
_____

It's like the old story of the blind men and the elephant. The trunk isn't the elephant, or the ear, or the tail. Yet the elephant wouldn't be itself without each of its parts. Likewise, a new couple cannot be understood by looking at just the husband or the wife. They are only parts of something bigger than themselves.

> The body is a unit,
> though it is made up of many parts;
> and though its parts are many,
> they form one body.
> 1 CORINTHIANS 12:12 NIV

Of course, without one of them there is no "couple" at all. Friends and families of a new couple will have to learn that they are now dealing with a new unit with new priorities. John may not be able to go to the game every weekend, and Mary may no longer call her parents twice a week, all because now they are "John and Mary."

Lord, help everyone affected by our marriage understand the changes
we will be going through as a new couple.
Right now we are so absorbed with each other that
we may overlook the feelings of our friends and family.
Give them patience and help them be happy for our happiness.

One of the first hurdles of any marriage is money. Before you married, you had your bills and he had his, and you dealt with them in your own ways. As a couple, you now have "our" debts, and "we" had better come to a fast agreement on how money should be handled. How you work it out is up to you, but work it out you must.

> Let no debt remain outstanding.
> ROMANS 13:8 NIV

You now have joint debts, in addition to individual ones, twice as many Christmas presents to buy, money to be saved and invested for children and retirement, insurance policies, and even a joint income-tax form. If you are unable to come up with a workable financial plan, get help from someone you trust.

Father, give us guidance in straightening out our financial life as a couple.
With Your help and some good advice from others, we can do this.

No one with any sense would walk up to a strange dog and grab it by the ears. You never know what the dog will do, but since its ears are very sensitive, an unpleasant scene is likely to result. Police officers hate domestic disturbance calls for the same reason: They can be dangerous to anyone who butts in.

> Like one who seizes a dog by the ears is a passer-by who meddles in a quarrel not his own.
> PROVERBS 26:17 NIV

You may think you're being helpful when you try to help someone else's marriage, but realize that both parties may turn on you.

Lord, teach us that while wanting to help others is an admirable trait,
a certain amount of caution is necessary.
If we're not careful, we will end up being hurt ourselves,
especially if the matter is none of our business.

> Like a bird that
> strays from its nest
> is a man who
> strays from his home.
> PROVERBS 27:8 NIV

We've been moved by their plight. Every spring misguided birds jump out of the nest before they master the art of flying and end up on the ground, where they usually die. We don't know why they do this, but it's a stupid move.

The same can be said for those who stray from their spouses. We can see them out there as they plummet to the ground in search of who knows what. We may even try to help, but we will usually fail to save them. We can't understand their actions any more than we can understand why baby birds take such fatal steps. All we can do is pity them.

Father, help us realize that we cannot save every baby bird or every sinner we come across. We can pray for them, but some things must be left in Your capable hands.

_____
_____
_____
_____
_____
_____
_____
_____
_____
_____
_____
_____
_____
_____
_____
_____

It's all in your intentions. There are perfectly good reasons for digging pits and rolling stones, as anyone who does backyard landscaping knows. But if you are digging a pit in hopes that your neighbor's dog will fall into it, or rolling a rock into the path of an oncoming vehicle, you will eventually get your comeuppance. How many pits have you dug this weekend for all the wrong reasons? How many rocks have you rolled into the path of others?

> If a man digs a pit,
> he will fall into it;
> if a man rolls a stone,
> it will roll back on him.
> PROVERBS 26:27 NIV

Father, there are many ways we can be stumbling blocks to others,
even if our intentions are innocent.
Show us when we may be hurting others
so we can become better witnesses for You.

You don't have to commit willful acts of violence to hurt others. Think back on the week that has just passed and look for the little things you did that may have been harmful to another. Were they honest mistakes, or was there a touch of anger in them? How can you become more sensitive to the needs of others? What can you do to make up for your mistakes? Don't beat yourself up over it, just try to be more sensitive next week.

Do you look in the mirror with some satisfaction, or do you only see that nose or those hips or that hair? On days when all you can see are your flaws, think about the one person you admire the most. If you were to be perfectly honest, would that person look good on a calendar for a whole month? Could he or she serve as an example of physical fitness and charm?

> And let the beauty of
> the LORD our God be upon us. . . .
> PSALM 90:17 NKJV

You don't admire Christians because of their physical beauty. You admire them because the beauty of God shines from within them, and such beauty is irresistible. Try showing the beauty of the Lord through your life, not through liposuction.

Lord, when we begin to worry too much about our outward appearance,
remind us that others see You in us,
and help us reflect that beauty in our lives.

My soul waits for the Lord more than those who watch for the morning.

PSALM 130:6 NKJV

If you have ever paced the night away with a crying baby, or suffered until dawn with a raging fever, you know what it means to watch for the morning. The baby may continue to scream through the dawn, and the sick may still be in pain, but there is something life-giving about witnessing the break of dawn. You made it to the start of a new day, and that brings hope.

Today could be better than yesterday. Yet that hope is nothing compared to the hope the Christian holds in the Lord, who will heal the sick and calm the young forever.

Father, thank You for the hope that a new day brings us,
which is only a taste of the hope we hold in You.

You've done it! You've purchased your first house after years of saving and maybe a little cash up front from your parents. You can afford the monthly payments and life is good. What you bought, of course, is just a house—wallboard and two-by-fours, electrical wires, and water pipes. Turning that structure into a home is up to you.

> Unless the LORD builds the house, they labor in vain who build it.
> PSALM 127:1 NKJV

Some mansions are never homes, while some of the most modest starter houses are homes from the first night you sleep there. Ask the Lord's blessing on your new home, and then furnish it with His love.

Father, we thank You for giving us the blessing of owning our own home.
May we live here in such a way that our lives and the home we make will reflect Your love.

> Do all things without murmuring and disputing, that you may become blameless and harmless, children of God without fault in the midst of a crooked and perverse generation, among whom you shine as lights in the world.
> PHILIPPIANS 2:14–15 NKJV

That's a pretty tall order. Most of the time we are able to live without murmuring and arguing, and we certainly try to be blameless and harmless, but "without fault"? We know we'll never quite reach that mark. And how are we supposed to be "lights in the world"? There isn't enough Windex on earth for that job.

Think for a moment about a lighthouse. Shining a powerful beam across the waters, this beacon of light does a pretty good job, even if its windows are salt-encrusted and it does nothing more than just stand there on the rocks. Sometimes that's all we need to do: stand faithfully on the Rock and shine the best we can.

Lord, You are the Rock we stand on.
Our light may not be perfect, but our foundation is sure.

We go through a lot of changes in our lives, some of which we try desperately to avoid, and all of which teach us something. Eating hot dogs and beans several times a week isn't fun, but we do learn that the most humble of diets can keep us alive. A long period of unemployment can take a house away from us, but we soon find we can survive in a tiny apartment, too.

> I know how to be abased, and I know how to abound. Everywhere and in all things I have learned both to be full and to be hungry, both to abound and to suffer need. I can do all things through Christ who strengthens me.
> PHILIPPIANS 4:12–13 NKJV

No one wants to go through hard times. We'd rather learn to abound and be full, but if God is with us, we can do anything. Perhaps the most important thing we can learn from hard times is that God stays with us through them all and brings us out of them in His time.

Father, Your constant and faithful love will bring us through any trial we may have to face.
When times are good again,
we will not forget the strength You gave us in our darkest moments.

SATURDAY

> Therefore,
> my beloved brethren,
> be steadfast, immovable,
> always abounding in the work of the Lord,
> knowing that your labor
> is not in vain in the Lord.
>
> 1 CORINTHIANS 15:58 NKJV

Often the world's motto seems to be "Nice guys finish last." The crude, the loud, and the ugly seem to be the winners in life, and not the faithful, the kind, and the considerate, who are walked over time and time again.

Paul knew this, having been walked over a few times himself, but still he said, "Your labor is not in vain." Being steadfast and immovable in working for the Lord may not result in measurable success, at least not right away. None of us knows why we were put here to do the work we do, but we labor on, trusting in God's perfect plan for our lives.

Father, when we become discouraged, keep us faithful.
When we become weak, make us strong.
When the world pulls our feet from under us, set them firmly on our Rock
so we may continue Your work here on earth.

This weekend why not think about signing up for some volunteer work in the church or community? With winter due to arrive in the near future, volunteering will keep cabin fever away from your door and give you a good reason to shovel the driveway. If you begin now, you will be well into your new "job" before winter, making a valuable contribution to your community. Some people have more available time than others, but there is work out there for everyone, regardless of time, talent, and personality.

And God is able to make
all grace abound toward you, that you,
always having all sufficiency in all things,
may have an abundance for
every good work.
2 CORINTHIANS 9:8 NKJV

Have you given up answering the telephone between 6:00 and 9:00 P.M., those three hours of prime telemarketing time? Once in a while someone you know calls, but most of the time it's "buy this," "donate that," and "pledge so much." Why don't they get the message and stop calling? Because charities and salespeople have found these methods work, that's why.

There is money available for good works even when you annoy everyone. Five dollars here and there do add up to "abundance."

Father, we are thankful that we have what we need to live on
and a little more to give to our favorite charities.
Our donation may not amount to much by itself,
but when added to those of others, it is enough.

_____

_____

_____

_____

_____

_____

_____

_____

_____

_____

_____

_____

_____

_____

Have you noticed that it's easier to forgive a stranger than a spouse? Unlike your partner, you aren't emotionally invested in a stranger. But when a husband or wife hurts you, you *really* hurt. Part of the pain comes from knowing that your spouse is well aware of exactly what will hurt you and uses that knowledge with intent.

> Bearing with one another,
> and forgiving one another,
> if anyone has a complaint against another;
> even as Christ forgave you,
> so you also must do.
> COLOSSIANS 3:13 NKJV

The Bible gives us no quarter here: "so you also must do." You *must* forgive each other and move on, for the sake of your witness and your marriage, no matter how betrayed you feel.

Lord, when we fight unfairly with each other and intentionally hurt each other,
give us the strength we need to forgive,
no matter how hard that is to do.

_____WEDNESDAY_____

> But above all. . .
> put on love,
> which is the bond of perfection.
> COLOSSIANS 3:14 NKJV

Why do over 50 percent of marriages end in divorce? More important, why do 50 percent of marriages endure for life? What do half of the people understand that the other half do not?

Maybe they understand the true nature of love. Love is always changing, never static. It grows and matures as we do. Love is giving, not taking, forgiving, not abandoning. As people change, so does the nature of their love, and passions flare and subside.

The wise person, however, understands change, and even welcomes the variety it brings to life. No, your spouse will not be twenty-five forever, but what fifty-year-old would want to live with someone who lacks the depth and wisdom to understand him?

Lord, help us adjust to the changing nature of love
and welcome its growth the same way we welcome the growth of a child.

When you come down to it, the Bible is a pretty realistic book, portraying the harshness of life and showing us how to deal with it. There will always be poor people in the land, but we are to open our hands wide to them.

We are told to reach into our pockets, pull out what we have, and give whatever is needed, not dribble a few coins out of a clenched fist while hiding the big bills. This isn't a suggestion, it's a command, and a pretty firm one at that. How we obey that command could very well determine the fate of the world.

"For the poor will never cease from the land; therefore I command you, saying, 'You shall open your hand wide to your brother, to your poor and your needy.'"
DEUTERONOMY 15:11 NKJV

Father, help us put our wishes and desires aside when faced with the poor and share our good fortune without grumbling or regret.

_____FRIDAY_____

> Do not marvel, my brethren,
> if the world hates you.
> 1 JOHN 3:13 NKJV

Christianity is not a popularity contest; it's a way of living that nonbelievers do not understand. After all, we fear what we don't understand, and we hate what we fear.

There you are, living a pretty good Christian life, when someone turns on you as if you were a dangerous animal. What's going on? What did you do wrong? You didn't do anything wrong; you did something not understandable, which caused fear, which brought hatred.

Sometimes explaining your beliefs helps, and sometimes it only makes things worse. You are what you are and need not apologize for your beliefs.

Father, when someone turns against us because of the way we live our lives,
help us understand his actions and give us the strength to continue to do right in Your eyes.

It's easy to say, "I love you," especially when we want something from another. The words just fall off our tongues, never even going through our brains on the way. You can fool a lot of people into believing those words, too, at least until your actions prove otherwise.

> My little children,
> let us not love in word or in tongue,
> but in deed and in truth.
> 1 JOHN 3:18 NKJV

Christians who have been brought up to love generously can be guilty of using those three words inappropriately, too. There are a lot of huggy-kissy Christians who would be well advised to keep their distance until others can see if their words are backed up by their lives.

Father, let us show our love to the world in practical, honest ways,
not in meaningless words that can be misunderstood or disbelieved.

_____SUNDAY_____

What's a football fan to do? It's the highlight of the week, coming home from church, changing into sweats, assembling the food and beverages, and then falling asleep on the couch in the third quarter. Sure it's a waste of time. That's the *idea*. All the rest of the week your time is not your own, but these three hours (barring overtime) are yours and yours alone. It's nice if your spouse and children understand this, but unusual. Maybe they would if you explained your need for that time or tried to educate them on the finer points of the game. Maybe not. Either way, enjoy the game.

What a testimony Joshua gave to God's faithfulness! Through all the years Joshua had led God's people, God had *never* failed them.

"Now I am about to go
the way of all the earth.
You know with all your heart
and soul that not one of
all the good promises
the LORD your God gave you has failed.
Every promise has been fulfilled."
JOSHUA 23:14 NIV

Sometimes our lives hold about as much turmoil as the Israelites'. We may not take up arms against a pagan nation, yet we often fight off sin and attacks from those who don't share our faith. Life can get pretty rough. Even in the thick of battle, though, we can remember Joshua's deathbed testimony: God has not failed us. He will fulfill every promise.

If we follow God's covenant—if we will be His people, He will be our God—we will prosper, despite all the enemies who come against us.

If we do that our whole lives, we will say with Joshua, "Every promise has been fulfilled."

Thank You, Lord, for Your faithfulness.
We seek to follow Your covenant every day of our lives.

> "Do you not say,
> 'There are still four months
> and then comes the harvest'?
> . . .Lift up your eyes
> and look at the fields,
> for they are already
> white for harvest!"
> JOHN 4:35 NKJV

Witnessing is uncomfortable for many of us. In an increasingly pagan world, it's hard to open our mouths with confidence, so we put off sharing our faith. *I'll mention God some other time,* we may decide, *when he might take it better.* Or we think, *She's just not ready and seeking yet,* though we really don't know that.

At harvest time, it's easy to see land producing a crop. Leave fruit on the tree too long and it will die. Nothing smells worse than rotting fruit—unless it's an unspoken witness. That's why Jesus warned His disciples that though spiritual harvests often aren't as obvious as the physical kind, people were still waiting to be picked.

Like the twelve disciples, we may be God's fruit "pickers." As we speak words of witness, ripe fruit may fall right into our hands.

Open our lips, Lord, with Your words of truth.
We want to cast aside the fears that keep us from witnessing to Your love.

There are no *"nos"* in God's promises. He never denies something He has said He will do or fails to follow through on a pledge He has made. Totally faithful to the words He has spoken, He comes through in the darkest moment or on the sunniest of days.

> For no matter how many promises God has made, they are "Yes" in Christ. And so through him the "Amen" is spoken by us to the glory of God.
> 2 CORINTHIANS 1:20 NIV

Friends may deny you, your boss may fire you, and your spouse may fail you. They're human, after all. And no human has unlimited control over life.

But the "yes" God says in Jesus doesn't change. Not only will He stand by you in this life, in the next life He will bring you to eternal life. His eternal "yes" lasts a lifetime, and not just through the latest rough patch.

Have you said "amen" to Jesus, the great Amen? Do you know His truth today?

Lord, You alone are the final truth,
the final yes that ends all nos. *Be the yes of our lives.*

> So I made up my mind that
> I would not make
> another painful visit to you.
> 2 CORINTHIANS 2:1 NIV

Some relationships are trouble from the start. You meet a person and just don't get on. If it's a casual acquaintance, you probably have a tacit agreement not to meet too often. It's better for you both that way.

But it's different when it's a family member, and especially difficult when it's someone in your spouse's family. If that person lives far away, you don't meet all that often and can work around it. But nearby relatives provide a greater challenge.

Perhaps you need to talk out an issue and come to an agreement. Make a try. But if that fails, don't feel you must spend a lot of time battling with a family member. That could ruin your witness for Christ.

Paul didn't force himself on the Corinthians after they had a painful visit. Neither did he give up on the church. Like Paul and the Corinthian church, place a little distance between you temporarily, spend time in prayer and thought, and things may gain a new perspective.

Even as Christians, we don't always agree with family.
Give us grace for those difficult relationships.

_____

_____

_____

_____

_____

_____

_____

_____

_____

_____

Need a cure for anxiety? Rejoice in God, knowing He is near you. How can you worry when the Lord of the universe is at your side?

> Rejoice in the Lord always. Again I will say, rejoice! . . .The Lord is at hand.
> PHILIPPIANS 4:4–5 NKJV

How often we worry because we're not focused on God and His ability to care for our troubles. We fret and fume, carrying our own load with great difficulty, instead of rejoicing that we have a God who cares enough to deal with our every burden.

When we focus on burdens instead of God's strength to carry them for us, God often lets us stew for a while. That way we begin to understand the pain of sin and turn from it.

Often, when we finally turn away from sin, we discover that God eliminates that trouble with one quick, simple act. What we thought was such a huge problem was nothing for the King of the universe.

Why didn't we turn to Him sooner?

Lord, here are our troubles.
Please bear this burden for us so we can rejoice in You.

> But if not,
> be it known unto thee, O king,
> that we will not serve thy gods,
> nor worship the golden image
> which thou hast set up.
> DANIEL 3:18 KJV

As Hitler's troops closed in on the isle of Jersey, a brief message went out to England: "But if not."

Unlike many today, those who received the message knew the meaning of the words from this verse found in the Book of Daniel. No matter what happened on Jersey, there would be brave people who would not bow the knee to the German dictator. Like Shadrach, Meshach, and Abednego, death threats would not keep them from doing right.

For all his efforts, Hitler never wiped out the European resistance, and finally, the Allied forces were victorious.

Like the three Hebrews who originally spoke the words of this verse, you may face powerful forces that would disobey God and want you to join them. Are you willing to say, "But if not"? It may not require your life but it may mean sacrifice. Are you ready today?

Lord, show us when we need to stand firm for You,
no matter the cost.

Has God been faithful to you in your Christian walk? Of course He has, even if you've only known Him a short while.

Today, with your spouse, share ways that you have seen God's faithfulness. Has He given you a new freedom in life, brought you through financial trials, or worked in a surprising way? If you have walked closely with the Lord for some time, you should have a good list.

Is there something you are worrying about today? Can you trust God to handle it? Discuss any problems you have with trusting God for faithfulness and come to Him in prayer.

Don't forget to rejoice in Him, while you pray.

"If it pleases the king,"
replied Esther,
"let the king, together with Haman,
come today to a banquet
I have prepared for him."
ESTHER 5:4 NIV

Queen Esther had a delicate subject to put before the king: His favorite minister had done wrong to her people, and she wanted redress.

Unlike many of us, Esther did not charge into the court, denounce her enemy, and expect a quick solution. She spoke tactfully, prepared the king, and then took action. Instead of making a fool of her enemy in public, she pleaded her case in private.

Sometimes we have a case to plead with someone. While we are angry and emotionally charged, we rush in to find redress—and are totally surprised when things don't go as we expected.

Because we have a just cause doesn't mean we should not use tact and wisdom in presenting our requests to others. When we do that, like Esther, we may win the day.

Lord, we don't want to be brash in our requests to You or people.
Show us how to act with tact and wisdom to plead our cases.

_____

_____

_____

_____

_____

_____

_____

_____

_____

_____

_____

_____

Wrong takes place in public, and people are afraid to stop it. Someone does an illegal act, and those who see it are afraid to make it public.

Mordecai wasn't one of those frightened folk who refuses to take action when danger threatens. He heard of a plot against his people and responded. After careful thought, no doubt, he encouraged his niece to tell her husband, a pagan king, of the plot. Mordecai knew his request could put his niece in danger, but truth was more important than danger.

> Mordecai the Jew was second in rank to King Xerxes, preeminent among the Jews, and held in high esteem by his many fellow Jews, because he worked for the good of his people and spoke up for the welfare of all the Jews.
> ESTHER 10:3 NIV

For doing right, Mordecai received honor from the king and his own people. Virtue got its just deserts.

When we see wrong, we, too, must plan and respond, though we won't become kings' counselors. Instead our actions will please the King.

When wrong faces us, Lord, give us courage to respond in Your truth.
Show us how we can rightly respond.

> "I will sweep away everything from the face of the earth," declares the LORD.
> ZEPHANIAH 1:2 NIV

A day is coming when God will set the world right. Instead of saving humanity in an ark, He will pronounce an ultimate judgment.

Most of us would like to see sin wiped out and righteousness rule. We'd like our enemies to realize they are wrong without suffering much. Still, the graphic imagery of Zephaniah's book seems unnecessarily unpleasant.

But God takes sin seriously. His goal is to eradicate all sin, something that can't be done with sweet phrases. God ruthlessly sweeps sin out of His people's lives and out of the world. Anything less would deny the immense price His Son paid on the cross to connect sinful people with Himself.

Sin isn't pleasant, and God never calls it that. But He's also not silent about its impact or ultimate end. He warned you to avoid an awful judgment. Have you listened? Have you shared that news with others?

Lord, we don't relish Your judgment, though we know it is just.
Help us to reach out to those who need to know You.

_____
_____
_____
_____
_____
_____
_____
_____
_____
_____
_____

The year of preparation for her meeting with the king must have held tense moments for Esther. A pagan leader suddenly had control of her life. If she pleased him, life might seem good—but what would marriage to a pagan be like? How could God have put her in this position?

> Now the king was attracted to Esther more than to any of the other women, and she won his favor and approval more than any of the other virgins.
> ESTHER 2:17 NIV

Sometimes we know how Esther felt. We face sin-filled situations that seem to have no rhyme or reason. Yet we remain in those messy spots, and God doesn't seem to call us out of them, even when we ask nicely.

Like Esther, we may be put in this place "for such a time as this" (v. 4:14). In a less-than-perfect situation, we may be God's only witness.

God made Esther appeal to the king, and hers was an effective witness. Soon we may see the purpose of God's timing in our lives.

We want to be effective witnesses for You, Lord,
even in imperfect situations.
Keep us in Your will.

_____ FRIDAY _____

> To him who is able
> to keep you from falling
> and to present you before
> his glorious presence without fault
> and with great joy.
> JUDE 24 NIV

Trying to obey God can be hard work. You have the best intentions but things keep going wrong. Even doing what is right doesn't seem to solve the problem. You're stuck.

Maybe you've started to rely on your own power. Getting caught up in dotting the i's and crossing the t's of faith traps you in legalism. Doing right isn't a matter of earning something with God but showing how much you love Him. Love needs to flow from appreciation, not obligation.

Oddly, you can't please God without God's power doing that work in your life. Try to please God on your own and you fail.

Jesus alone makes you perfect and presents you to the Father in a spotless white robe, pure and undefiled. You can't put on that robe under your own power or enter God's glorious throne room without Him. Share that joy with Him by letting Him work in you.

Lord, we want to appreciate You, not feel obligated.
Work in our lives today.

_____

_____

_____

_____

_____

_____

_____

_____

_____

_____

_____

If we are valuable people—and we are—it's not because of our efforts. Left to our own devices, we fall into sin, make wrong choices, and mess up our lives. Hard as we try, we just can't seem to get things straight.

> As His divine power has given to us all things that pertain to life and godliness, through the knowledge of Him who called us by glory and virtue.
> 2 PETER 1:3 NKJV

Any glory and virtue we show come from the One who exhibits those attributes perfectly: Jesus. When we couldn't get things straight, He came into our lives and redesigned them. Out of the dusty, bumpy deserts of our lives, He made a highway leading straight to God (see Isaiah 40:3). Without Him, we'd never have built that thoroughfare. Some of us have spent a lot of time traveling on dusty, dirty paths that led nowhere.

Are you sharing His life and godliness, or are you lost, wandering down your own dusty path?

Lord, Your power working through us brings us to the place we want to be.
Thank You for sharing it with us.

Martyrs, missionaries, and other committed Christians have made great sacrifices for the Gospel. Theirs has been a powerful testimony for God.

This weekend, stop by a library, visit a Christian bookstore, or surf the Internet and learn some more about such admirable Christians as Eric Liddell, Jim Elliot, Corrie ten Boom, and William Carey. Or look up heroes such as Jan Hus and William Tyndale. (There are many Christian heroes and heroines who can impact your faith.)

Together, discuss these people and how their lives can influence yours. Why do you admire them? How can you better serve God by knowing their testimonies?

_____

_____

_____

_____

_____

_____

_____

_____

_____

_____

_____

A monarch is coming: Jesus is on His way. Will He climb into your lives over boulders, down deep crevices, and up the other side again? Or will He be able to reach your hearts on a fairly smooth path?

> The voice of him that crieth in the wilderness, Prepare ye the way of the LORD, make straight in the desert a highway for our God.
> ISAIAH 40:3 KJV

All of us have some bumps in the road. Under our own power, we can't design a flat highway that avoids hairpin turns and deep divides. But we can make sure the boulders of sin don't take over our lives. By coming to Christ each day, confessing sin, and seeking to do His will, we can help clear the path. Then He can start reengineering our lives. Only He can design a highway that bridges the divides and takes the turns safely.

Who is engineering your path—you or God?

Lord, we want You to have smooth access to our lives. Take the boulders of sin away and smooth our ways.

> Go ye therefore
> into the highways,
> and as many as ye shall find,
> bid to the marriage.
> MATTHEW 22:9 KJV

Highways can be rather scary places. Plenty of law-abiding citizens travel them, but so do the riffraff of society—dangerous people you'd rather not encounter.

Jesus didn't limit His ministry to only the fine folks of Israel. Yes, He invited princes and kings and the well-to-do ladies into His kingdom, but Jesus also called the outcasts, the people from "the other side of town" or with the "wrong" ethnic background. He sought out the dangerous people on the highways.

Like the king in this parable, the King of the universe has been spurned by some of the "best" folks in town. That doesn't stop Him.

It isn't how well we're dressed or what money we have that matters to Jesus. He looks on the heart. A beggar who turns to Him becomes rich, while a rich man who spurns Him is poor all his life.

Thank You, Lord, for the richness of Your calling.
You took us off life's highway and brought us to Your feast.

When afflictions surround us, our path seems cut into stone. We can't seem to change direction, and we always seem to take the longest path to anywhere. We're blocked in by circumstances. We're no longer on a highway but a crooked little trail that seems to go nowhere.

> He hath inclosed my ways with hewn stone, he hath made my paths crooked.
>
> LAMENTATIONS 3:9 KJV

Like the prophet, we feel frustration. *Why does God have us here?* we may wonder. It just doesn't seem to make sense.

Not all of God's ways are highways. Sometimes, to fulfill His will, He has to bring you down a side path of trouble. But in the end, by following His way, you'll be able to glorify God. He has not forgotten you. "His compassions fail not," testifies the prophet (v. 22). Hope lies just around the corner, when you serve God.

Even the narrowest path leads to Him when you follow His will.

Lord, we know Your compassion hasn't failed us,
even when the road is long and narrow.
Thank You for leading us in Your way, even when it's a hard path.

> Is not my word
> like as a fire? saith the LORD;
> and like a hammer that
> breaketh the rock in pieces?
> JEREMIAH 23:29 KJV

God's Word—whether written in the Bible or spoken —is powerful. To misrepresent it is to misrepresent His will and way. Those who do so may seem prosperous for a time, but God does not take their misdeeds lightly. One day they will be destroyed as if a hammer had pounded them in pieces.

When we speak about God's Word to each other, do we treat it respectfully or try to make it say whatever we want to hear? If we don't treat it with reverence, looking to see what God really has to say to us, we are like the false prophets Jeremiah dealt with. God is against such people and will see that they don't prosper.

Prosper today by listening carefully to God's Word and acting it out in your lives. Then the flame of His love will burn in your hearts and not destroy you.

Lord, let Your Spirit burn brightly in our hearts as we revere You and seek Your will through Your Word.

You've planned a ministry together or in your church, but the money just doesn't seem to be in the budget. Should you or your church go into debt to make it happen?

> "'The silver is mine and the gold is mine,' declares the Lord Almighty."
> HAGGAI 2:8 NIV

One way God weeds out those ministries that are not His is to let them languish financially. People who get involved in otherwise godly things to make themselves look good will often run into financial troubles that end up wrecking their ministries.

That doesn't mean that every accounting problem is a sign that you're out of God's will. Sometimes it's just a test to make sure you're keeping your eyes on God and not seeking your own fame or the appreciation of others.

God owns all the money in the world. He will provide for that ministry He has in mind. Just tune in to Him and be clear that you're doing His will. He will provide a way.

Lord, we want to serve You, not gain kudos for ourselves.
Whether it's a formal ministry or just the witness of our lives,
let our actions glorify You.

> Return to the LORD your God,
> for he is gracious and compassionate,
> slow to anger and abounding in love,
> and he relents from sending calamity.
>
> JOEL 2:13 NIV

When God's people turn from Him, He does not immediately explode in anger. First, He calls them to repent and enjoy the relationship He's always wanted to share with them. Over the course of history, those who believe in Him have sometimes obeyed, and sometimes they have not.

If you've been married more than a short while, chances are you know how God feels. You want a close relationship with your spouse. You'd like to keep that honeymoon feeling forever. But it doesn't work that way. Sin always works into a marriage after time. Perhaps it's that irritating habit you never mentioned while you were dating or a lack of consideration that never occurred before marriage.

Seek forgiveness and healing together, instead of indulging in anger and calamities, and your relationship can deepen. You can't live on honeymoon love forever, but you can keep calamities at bay.

Lord, help us to seek forgiveness, not anger, as our first reaction.
We want healing, not calamity, in our love.

_____

_____

_____

_____

_____

_____

_____

_____

_____

_____

_____

_____

_____

_____

_____

_____

_____

Are you experiencing bumps in your path or are you driving along a smooth highway? As a Christian, you can be sure to travel on both surfaces of life. What does it all mean? Can bumps be signs that you need to draw closer to God?

While things may be going along blissfully, "smooth highways" don't always mean you are right in God's will. Often very powerful Christians who are walking in God's will go through serious trials. Then again, some purely nominal Christians have lives of ease.

Which of these descriptions best fits you? If you have trials, are they the result of sin in your lives or obedience that has led you down a difficult path?

Discuss the path you are on right now. Do you need to turn around and go in another direction, walk more closely with God, or stay in your current direction? Do you need to make a turn that you've avoided so far?

> Because of the truth,
> which lives in us
> and will be with us forever.
> 2 JOHN 2 NIV

Try getting away from the truth, as a Christian, and you'll find it's still with you. Why? Because truth lives in you through Jesus, not just today but forever. You can't evade truth, and why should you? Being close to Jesus and knowing how He wants you to live gives you a wonderful life.

Living with lies messes up life, as even those of us who slip into untruths occasionally can testify. We may lie to gain some benefits and discover they're short-lived, if they come at all.

The results of lying aren't what we think they will be. We expect less trouble by evading truth, but end up in more. If we make lying a life habit, we may seem to win in the short run, but we'll gain bad reputations and see many disasters in our lives.

God does repay lying—with trouble and spiritual death. If that's a harvest you don't want, don't do it!

Lord, You are truth. Keep living in us.

Do you tell the truth to your spouse? You should.
After all, isn't he or she your closest neighbor?
You truly are members one of another, even
more closely connected to each other than to
Christian brothers and sisters.

> Wherefore putting away lying,
> speak every man truth
> with his neighbour:
> for we are members
> one of another.
> EPHESIANS 4:25 KJV

   Living with a person who doesn't tell the
truth is extremely aggravating. How do you know
what to believe, when that person sometimes says
what is so and sometimes doesn't? Instead of drawing closer, a couple will be divided by lies.
Anger is likely to be their constant companion because one will hate being lied to and the
other won't understand what the problem is.

   If you want to be members of one another, you can't live with constant lies. Truth draws
you closer as you trust each other. So, put away those lies from your home as well as your
church life.

Lord, we want to speak the truth to each other.
Help us to put away those lies and trust each other.

As we continue on our Christian walks, we're sure to be confronted by people who have different beliefs. Sometimes those beliefs are a reasonable disagreement between two ways of thinking about God. Christians honestly differ on some minor points of doctrine.

> You were running a good race. Who cut in on you and kept you from obeying the truth?
>
> GALATIANS 5:7 NIV

But there are also those who would like to draw us away from the race for truth and into empty, man-made courses of argument.

Not only do we need to learn the truth, we need to "keep on keeping on" in it. Instead of falling for convoluted arguments that run us in circles or appeal to our baser instincts, we must continue on in the right direction.

God has given us a clear "truth map" in His Word and through His leading Spirit. We just have to run the race according to His directions.

Lord, it's so easy to be distracted from Your truth.
Keep our hearts and eyes on You so that we may
become lights to guide others in Your way.

Can you imagine starting a contracting project and being so convinced of the workers' honesty that you didn't even require bills or financial proofs of any kind? That would be one unusual contractor!

> They did not require an accounting from those to whom they gave the money to pay the workers, because they acted with complete honesty.
> 2 KINGS 12:15 NIV

But the priests involved in building the temple were this trusting. They didn't need to see the paperwork. They had hired honest workers who also knew that God was watching over their labors and who feared offending Him.

Are you like those builders? You may work with computers instead of hammers and awls, but God still sees your work and wants to direct it. When you are honest with clients or customers, He sees that. When you aren't, He sees that, too.

If your boss required no accounting of time or money from you, could you honestly stand before God?

Lord, we want to be workers worthy of Your hire.
We want to be honest in all we do.

_____ FRIDAY _____

> "Let God weigh me in honest scales and he will know that I am blameless."
> JOB 31:6 NIV

Job felt God was being unfair. After doing his best to obey Him, the rich man was being called sinful by a bunch of legalists who called themselves "friends."

Job made sacrifices every morning in case unidentified sin had entered his household (1:5). Even God called him blameless (1:8). What more was needed?

A lot more. What upright man can claim complete blamelessness? As hard as any of us tries to obey God, our slippery natures ease us into sin. Job's sins were covered by sacrifices, not by his own sinless nature. Without sacrifices, he could never have claimed purity.

The perfection Job needed was what Jesus died to bring humanity—until that day, animal sacrifice was the temporary solution.

If God weighed us on Job's "honest" scales, comparing us to Jesus, could we be blameless? No. Instead, we'd claim the one-time sacrifice of the Blameless One.

Thank You, Jesus, for taking our sin and making us blameless through Your sacrifice.

Some people treat anger as a weapon. To manipulate others to their ways, they attack with sharp words or even physical violence.

> The LORD is slow to anger and great in power, and will not at all acquit the wicked.
> NAHUM 1:3 NKJV

Such reactions do not show a person's power but his weakness. A truly powerful person follows God in being slow to anger. But that does not mean a wrongdoer always gets away with evil. It just means rushed reactions are not a good thing.

As humans, we usually want quick results: judgment for the evildoer, at any cost. God promises to bring justice to every situation—but not on our time schedule or in our way.

We can trust in the God who is slow to anger because we have experienced His mercy. When we err or even sin intentionally, He is also slow to retaliate so that we can have time to come to Him in repentance.

Aren't we all glad swift justice is not always His?

Thank You, Lord, for being slow to anger.
Teach us also to consider well before we open our mouths in judgment.

Read Job 31. Is Job being honest? Is this good man perfect? Read what God says in Job 40:2 and Job's response in the next verse and 42:1–6. Was God weighing him in honest scales? What didn't Job understand?

Is honesty important in your marriage? Do you appreciate your spouse's honesty?

When does honesty go too far? Think of a case in your own life when you were too honest with someone or someone hurt you with honesty. What could have been done better?

How do you find a balance between honesty and tact? Do you need to seek God for help in this area?

When trouble comes, do you look to your check-book, job security, or your spouse for protection?

The LORD is good,
a stronghold in the day of trouble;
and He knows those who
trust in Him.
NAHUM 1:7 NKJV

We all hope those things remain solid, but the truth is that at some time, each can fail us. Money may not last, a job may disappear, and our spouses make mistakes. We can't always lean on them because they are earthly. The things that affect us affect them, too.

We need a refuge greater than the world, one that can stand up to it. As long as we look to earth for security, it evades us. Our stronghold, Nahum reminds us, can only be God. We can trust His goodness that even when He rains down judgment on those around us, He will not forget His children. We remain safe in His citadel when the world around us comes breaking apart.

Run to those arms. Enter the gates of the stronghold where you are known and pro-tected. No enemy harms you there.

Thank You, Lord God, for being our protection.
Keep us fast through all our trials.

> Israel is an empty vine,
> he bringeth forth fruit unto himself:
> according to the multitude of
> his fruit he hath increased his altars;
> according to the goodness of his land
> they have made goodly images.
> HOSEA 10:1 KJV

Emptiness fills those who turn away from God. They may crowd churches, but worshiping their own goodness and insisting on barren theologies leaves them empty, no matter how packed the sanctuary.

When we bring forth our own fruit, designed by us instead of God, we worship at altars that are not His. Many hurting people have run to spiritually empty congregations and thought they've heard from God. No wonder these folks deny His power. False images have led them to ascribe to God something that has nothing to do with Him.

God's fruit isn't empty, though. When we worship at His altar, our theology isn't barren. God brings fullness to His people's lives when we set aside images of other gods and seek to serve Him alone.

Are you wholeheartedly serving Him today?

Lord, turn us from empty altars and toward true worship of You.

"The Bohemian disease" was what he was accused of having, but Martin Luther wasn't sick. In fact, he was one of the most spiritually well men in all of Europe.

His "disease" was that he agreed with the ideas of the fourteenth-century priest Jan Hus, a Bohemian who had pushed for church reform. John Wycliffe, the English Bible translator, had influenced Hus, and all three men seriously studied the Scriptures. Where the Bible and church practice didn't agree, they confronted a reluctant church.

> Then I heard the voice of the Lord saying, "Whom shall I send? And who will go for us?" And I said, "Here am I. Send me!"
> ISAIAH 6:8 NIV

The Reformation that sprang out of Luther's Ninety-five Theses, posted on this day in 1517, was not the work of one man. A long line of churchmen had faithfully studied Scripture and responded to its commands. For many, saying "Here am I; send me" to God had resulted in excommunication and even death.

When you read Scripture, can you say, "Send us"? You could be part of that line of faithful servants.

Lord, we want to serve You with whole hearts, no matter what it costs.

_____THURSDAY_____

> And Moses answered and said,
> But, behold, they will not believe me,
> nor hearken unto my voice:
> for they will say,
> The Lord hath not appeared unto thee.
> EXODUS 4:1 KJV

If you have teenage children, you will often feel like Moses. At the precise time of life they most need your guidance and advice, they stop listening.

They no longer have the unquestioning faith in you that they had at age five. This is the time for them to question anyone in authority, especially their parents. As aggravating as it can be, teenagers need to think things through for themselves, to build their own values and claim their own territory as individuals. They need to say, "*This* is what I believe."

They won't emerge from this period as carbon copies of you. And who would want them to be? They emerge as themselves, the unique people they want to be for the rest of their lives.

Father, during these emotional and trying years, please be there for our children. Guide them as they explore their own identities, and give us confidence that they will turn out to be the wonderful people they have the power to be, with Your help.

_____

_____

_____

_____

_____

_____

_____

_____

_____

_____

_____

_____

_____

_____

If we have a good marriage, we find it is difficult to accept this verse. Sure, we want to be like the angels, but it's nearly impossible to think of eternity without our spouses. Will we at least remember each other and the life we've had together? Will we still love each other?

> For when they shall rise from the dead, they neither marry, nor are given in marriage; but are as the angels which are in heaven.
>
> MARK 12:25 KJV

Our problem is that we know so little about eternity, and even less about angels. We are emotionally tied to what we know and afraid to give up what we have, even though God promises we will be happy. All we can know for sure is that God is a God of love.

Father, we know that You have only the best in mind for our future and that being with You will be more wonderful than we can possibly imagine. Calm our fears and lead us to trust Your plan.

_____SATURDAY_____

> That ye all speak the same thing,
> and that there be no divisions among you;
> but that ye be perfectly joined together
> in the same mind and
> in the same judgment.
> 1 CORINTHIANS 1:10 KJV

Do your children play you and your spouse off each other to get what they want? If Dad gives the "wrong" answer, they go talk to Mom, hoping for a better result. You have to learn to outflank them, to refuse to make the decision before the two of you talk about it, especially if it's an important one. Sometimes a conversation isn't needed and you can give your answer after just looking at your spouse. Sometimes you will disagree and have to work out a mutually acceptable compromise. At other times you will give a quick answer on your own, knowing what your spouse will say. The trick is not to let your children divide you, to be "in the same mind and in the same judgment."

Lord, our children need consistency, and we need to support each other in our decisions. Help us to be of one mind, for the sake of our children.

This weekend plan ahead a little and play "What if?" What if your son asked to borrow the car on Saturday night? What would you both say to that request? What if your daughter thought it was time to wear makeup? What if they both decided not to attend church? You can't anticipate every possible situation, but you do need to agree on the major ones, hopefully before they come up in real life.

> Then said the LORD,
> Doest thou well to be angry?
> JONAH 4:4 KJV

Jonah had predicted disaster, but God acted with mercy, contradicted Jonah's prophecy, and left him looking like a fool. Jonah was ticked off, to put it mildly. Then God asked if it was a good idea to be angry, given the situation.

People make fools of us all the time, changing their minds, contradicting our decisions, doing whatever they want in spite of our good advice. Our feelings are hurt and our reputations may even be damaged, but what good does it do to be angry? The decision has been taken out of our hands, and all we can do is move on.

Lord, when someone makes us look foolish,
help us control our unproductive anger,
knowing that You have everything under control
and things will all work out the way they were meant to work out.

Perhaps things haven't been going very well in your marriage recently. You haven't "dealt treacherously" with each other, but you haven't felt particularly loving either. Such "cool" phases happen in the best of marriages.

Now is a good time to remember that a marriage concerns three people, not two, and that the Lord gave you your spouse and knows exactly how you feel. He wants your marriage to thrive. Give Him time to help you. Don't toss away a gift of God.

> The LORD hath been witness between thee and the wife of thy youth, against whom thou hast dealt treacherously: yet is she thy companion, and the wife of thy covenant.
>
> MALACHI 2:14 KJV

Lord, when things go sour in our relationship,
give us the patience and determination we need to hang in there
and work things out between us with Your help.

> I have no greater joy than to hear that my children walk in truth.
> 3 JOHN 4 KJV

Somewhere along the line it will dawn on you that your children are now adults and it's time to "butt out." They aren't perfect yet, but neither are you. You did the best you could for them and have much to be proud of. They are not only functioning adults, but they also turned out to be talented, compassionate, faithful, and whatever other good qualities you see in them.

If they would let you, you would be proud to be their friend. This is your reward for all those hard years of work and worry. If they still need to improve here and there, you've got a few years left to work on them.

Father, thank You for helping our children grow into competent adults who no longer need or want our daily supervision. We're proud of them all and never could have gotten this far without Your help.

Felix didn't want to hear any more from Paul. What he had heard of the Gospel upset him, so he put off making any decision until a more "convenient" time.

> Go thy way for this time; when I have a convenient season, I will call for thee.
> ACTS 24:25 KJV

Procrastination is always the easiest way out. We do it all the time. "Shouldn't we volunteer to teach Sunday school?" "Let's wait and see if they really need us." "Did you talk to Junior about drugs?" "He's too young. Next year."

Sometimes we do need more time to make important decisions, and at other times we just put off important actions out of fear or distaste. The trick is in knowing when you really need to think something through and when you're just copping out.

Lord, help us make decisions when they need to be made,
not put them off until a more "convenient" time.

Therefore
if thine enemy hunger,
feed him;
if he thirst, give him drink. . . .
Be not overcome of evil,
but overcome evil with good.
ROMANS 12:20–21 KJV

It's so easy to be overcome by evil. When someone treats us poorly, we either fight or flee. It's a natural reaction to strike back or just get away before any more damage can be done.

But we have a third choice that we rarely even consider: We can overcome evil with good. We can stand our ground, smile politely, and treat our enemies with love and consideration. If we keep it up, they'll either leave us alone or begin to change their minds about us.

Let's give them something more worthwhile to think about.

Father, when someone strikes out at us,
give us the strength to answer hatred with love and aggression with peace.

To *covet* means to feel unreasonable desire for something that belongs to another. It's more than just wishing for a new car when your neighbor drives one home. You want *that* car, the one your neighbor has, not one just like it. And you want it badly. You can see how this can cause a lot of problems, especially if you covet your neighbor's wife!

Neither shalt thou desire thy neighbour's wife, neither shalt thou covet thy neighbour's house, his field, or his manservant, or his maidservant, his ox, or his ass, or any thing that is thy neighbour's.
DEUTERONOMY 5:21 KJV

The Lord knows we all have wishes and dreams, but He wants us to have the right perspective on them, and not let them control our lives or make us act irrationally. Wish for anything you want; covet nothing.

Lord, help us keep our desires and dreams under control,
knowing You will provide for us and give us the joy of answered prayers.

It's time to prepare for winter before the first snowfall drops in unannounced. The lawn needs one more raking before the leaves are permanently buried in snow; fireplace wood needs splitting; the cupboard needs to be stocked with "blizzard food"; and the batteries in the flashlight need changing, especially if the power tends to go off with the first snowflake. What do you need to do this weekend to be ready for winter?

We all know generous souls who require only one reward for their charity: recognition. Some are satisfied with a simple thank-you, while others want their names on a building or a mention of their gift from the pulpit. They're really not asking for much, and we can understand how they feel, but they are seeking a limited human reward.

> But when you give to the needy,
> do not let your left hand know
> what your right hand is doing,
> so that your giving may be in secret.
> Then your Father,
> who sees what is done in secret,
> will reward you.
> MATTHEW 6:3–4 NIV

God promises them much more if they keep their gifts a secret. The next time you give of your resources, try doing so in secret and see how much more rewarding your gift will feel to you.

Father, we know Your rewards are far greater than
anything we could receive from others.
Help us seek to please You with our gifts,
not our friends and neighbors.

God doesn't like punishing us any more than we enjoy punishing our children. The truth is, sometimes we need correction.

When was the last time you had to punish your children? You tried everything else you could think of first, but nothing worked. You couldn't get their attention any other way, and, as trite as it sounds, it did hurt you more than it hurt them.

The next time you feel that God might be punishing you, take time to figure out why. Have there been inner warnings you ignored? Confess your sins and know they will be forgiven.

> For men are not
> cast off by the Lord forever.
> Though he brings grief,
> he will show compassion,
> so great is his unfailing love.
> For he does not willingly bring affliction
> or grief to the children of men.
> LAMENTATIONS 3:31–33 NIV

Father, You may correct us when we stray from Your way,
but Your love is never-ending,
and You will never punish us unfairly.

The queen of Sheba was much like today's woman. She had heard wonderful things about a man— someone probably even told her he had a great personality! —but she had her own questions. He was rich and powerful, but so were a lot of bums, then and now. He had to prove himself to her before she would believe half the things others said.

> When the queen of Sheba heard of Solomon's fame, she came to Jerusalem to test him with hard questions.
> 2 CHRONICLES 9:1 NIV

Women do the same thing today, ignoring the outer trappings of a man and asking the hard questions that determine the fate of a relationship. Solomon passed the test, as you did if you are married. Give thanks to the Lord for the wisdom He has given you and the love that wisdom brought you.

Father, thank You for helping us find each other
and giving us the wisdom we needed to pass the tests of courtship.

> Be sure you know
> the condition of your flocks,
> give careful attention to your herds;
> for riches do not
> endure forever. . . .
> PROVERBS 27:23–24 NIV

Right now things may be going pretty well for you. Your promotion came through with a healthy raise and there's finally extra money in your checkbook. Great! Enjoy it, but don't forget what it took to get to this point.

You got that promotion because you faithfully attended to the nuts and bolts of your previous position, all those little details that no one else wanted to handle. If you want to keep advancing, you have to keep after those same details—plus those of your new position. Don't get so wrapped up in your own glory that you neglect what made you successful in the first place.

Lord, thank You for the talents You have given us and their rewards,
but keep us mindful of how we got where we are today.

Sooner or later, we all become orphans. It's devastating to wake up one morning knowing our parents are not just a telephone call away, and knowing, too, that they will never see any future grandchildren. We feel so lonely. We're never ready to stop being someone's beloved child. Other members of the older generation, aunts and uncles, can ease some of our pain, but soon they will be gone, too.

"I will be a Father to you, and you will be my sons and daughters, says the Lord Almighty."
2 CORINTHIANS 6:18 NIV

If you are facing times like these, accept God's offer to be your Father. Bring your problems to Him, listen for His advice, and know you are still loved.

Father, help us through these difficult times of being suddenly alone in the world. Pour Your love upon us as we turn to You in our grief.

> "Ask the former generations
> and find out what
> their fathers learned,
> for we were born only yesterday
> and know nothing."
>
> JOB 8:8–9 NIV

Reinventing the wheel is a terrible waste of time, and living without understanding the past only dooms us to future mistakes that could be avoided. Why go around and around in the same circle when your elders have already done that lap and can show you a shortcut?

Today information is readily available on almost any subject—more information than we can ever process ourselves. We need to know what information is useful and profitable and what is just junk. Ask those who have already been there, done that.

Father, our individual lives are short,
but collectively we have ages of wisdom and history to help us.
Give us the grace to listen to our elders and help humanity move forward,
with Your guidance.

How much do you know of your family history? What talents do you have that reflect those of a distant relative? Who you are is, in a large part, based on who your ancestors are, and in understanding them you will also understand yourself. This weekend talk to your elders about your family. When did they or the generation before come to this country? Where did they live, and why did they come? How many cousins are out there you don't know about, and how can you reach them? Knowing these things will connect you to the past, make you feel part of something bigger than yourself, and give you a valuable new perspective on life.

> Let no one say
> when he is tempted,
> "I am tempted by God";
> for God cannot be tempted by evil,
> nor does He Himself tempt anyone.
> But each one is tempted when
> he is drawn away by his own desires
> and enticed.
>
> JAMES 1:13–14 NKJV

The start of the holiday season is a good time to reflect on temptation. We need to shore ourselves up in the face of all the food, shopping, gift-giving, and plain old excess the holidays bring. It's always tempting to ignore our diets, spend more than we can afford, and otherwise get carried away at this time of year. Then we look for someone else to blame when the bills come in or when we step on the scales.

Today's verse warns us not to put the blame on God but to acknowledge that we can be our own worst enemies, giving in to our own desires and allowing ourselves to be enticed. This season, ask God for self-control, but take responsibility for your own actions.

Father, we know You never tempt us and can help us in our struggle.
This holiday season we ask You to stay by our sides and keep us strong,
whatever the temptation.

With a worldwide increase of interest in spirituality of all types, Christians need to keep on their toes to discern the truth. Some proponents of these spiritual movements sound logical and good, so how can you tell a false prophet from a real one? Granted, a false prophet is unmasked by his errors, but it could be years before he's proven wrong. What do you do in the meantime?

> Beloved,
> do not believe every spirit,
> but test the spirits,
> whether they are of God;
> because many false prophets
> have gone out into the world.
> By this you know the Spirit of God:
> Every spirit that confesses that Jesus Christ
> has come in the flesh is of God.
>
> 1 JOHN 4:1–2 NKJV

The best way to avoid becoming enmeshed in heresy is to ask one simple question: Does the person, movement, or philosophy espouse Jesus as the Savior? If not, back off and have nothing to do with such thinking.

*Father, give us the ability to discern the truth when we hear it
and avoid following anyone who does not come in the name of Your Son.*

**Yet He sets the poor on high,
far from affliction,
and makes their families like a flock.**

PSALM 107:41 NKJV

Today or early tomorrow you will join your own "flock" to celebrate Thanksgiving, even if that means spending hours in traffic or an airline terminal. Then, when you finally get there, you will have to deal with your family—those you really want to see and those you normally go to great lengths to avoid. You'll eat too much, stay up too late, and then make the long trip back to your normal life.

Some years spending time together doesn't seem worth the effort, but you will go because you are family, and having a family is one of the best of God's blessings.

*Lord, this year help us look on gathering with our family as a happy occasion,
not something to be endured.
You have made these people part of our lives for a reason,
and we thank You for all of them.*

We often forget that the Lord loves a holy ruckus. We think He likes things quiet and serene, people properly dressed, and hymns sung with restraint, so that's what we try to provide for Thanksgiving Day. Of course we never quite live up to our expectations, but who's to say that's bad?

Is it better for Grandpa to sleep alone in his chair or be mobbed by toddlers? Is it bad if the baby is louder than the football game on television? Is anyone going to get horribly ill if the turkey misses the platter and ends up on the floor? Families are loud when they're happy, and maybe God enjoys that, too.

Make a joyful shout
to the LORD, all you lands!
Serve the LORD with gladness:
Come before
His presence with singing.
Know that the LORD,
He is God.
PSALM 100:1–3 NKJV

Father, we often try to behave the way we think You would like us to,
but we can never know Your mind.
This year we will be as loud and ragged as always,
hoping our celebration pleases You as much as it pleases us.

FRIDAY

> Though the fig tree
> may not blossom,
> nor fruit be on the vines;
> though the labor of the olive may fail,
> and the fields yield no food;
> though the flock be cut off from the fold,
> and there be no herd in the stalls—
> yet I will rejoice in the LORD,
> I will joy in the God of my salvation.
>
> HABAKKUK 3:17–18 NKJV

Now that's a bad year! There was absolutely nothing to harvest—no fruits, no vegetables, no meat, no milk. People without supermarkets or credit were going to starve until the next harvest, if there was a next harvest. Yet still this farmer was going to rejoice in the God that saved him.

Have you had a bad year? Was it as bad as this fellow's? What did you have this year that you can celebrate and give thanks for?

Lord, no matter how bad the year has been, we will still rejoice.
You have saved us in body and in soul.

There is always danger in extremes. If we're rich, we tend to take the credit for our own success and not give it to God to whom it belongs. If we're poor, we may sin in desperation and dishonor the God we claim to follow. Neither extreme is a good witness to others.

Give me neither poverty nor riches—
Feed me with the food You prescribe for me;
lest I be full and deny You, and say,
"Who is the LORD?"
Or lest I be poor and steal,
and profane the name of my God.
PROVERBS 30:8–9 NKJV

Fortunately, most of us are somewhere between the two extremes of wealth and poverty, neither denying God's work in our lives nor profaning His name through our actions. It's a thin line we walk, but God will help us keep our balance.

Father, we thank You for all the blessings You have given us,
whether they are many or few.
May we live our lives in such a way that
others will see You in our lives and believe.

Before you get totally wrapped up in Christmas shopping and your children write their ten-page letters to Santa, try another type of list. This weekend get everyone together to compose a list of the year's blessings—things you have already received, not things you want. If making that list turns out to be enjoyable, go on to another and make a list of things you would like to give others this year. Not toys or jewelry, but loving acts of concern such as volunteering at the food bank, collecting gifts for homeless children, or donating to a cause that has touched your family this year. These lists can put the holiday in the right perspective for yourselves and your children.

It's easy to offer our gifts to the Father. It makes us feel good to be at peace with Him and contribute our time and money to the work of the church. But Jesus reminds us that in order to be at peace with Him, we first need to be at peace with our brothers and sisters. This is not a simple matter.

Who is your brother, and how have you wronged him? The wider you define the word *brother*, the more impossible the job becomes. Surely you can't be expected to resolve centuries of slavery, oppression, and wrongdoing on your own—can you? Seek God's guidance on this confusing matter and follow His leading.

> Therefore if thou bring thy gift to the altar, and there rememberest that thy brother hath ought against thee; leave there thy gift before the altar, and go thy way; first be reconciled to thy brother, and then come and offer thy gift.
> MATTHEW 5:23–24 KJV

*Father, show us where we have wronged others
and what we can do to be reconciled with them,
then give us the courage to do Your will in this world.*

Week 48

_____TUESDAY_____

> Take therefore
> no thought for the morrow:
> for the morrow shall take
> thought for the things of itself.
> Sufficient unto the day is the evil thereof.
> MATTHEW 6:34 KJV

Most of us are born worriers. Some things we can handle fairly well, while others keep us awake all night. If things are going fairly well one day, we still lie awake waiting for the second shoe to drop, knowing it *will* drop, wondering if we will survive the fall.

This is exactly what Jesus warns against: anticipatory worrying. Life provides us with plenty to deal with in one day, so why look ahead to tomorrow's problems? God knows exactly what we need and will provide it when we need it. That should leave us all with a little extra time to "seek first the kingdom of God, and his righteousness" (Matthew 6:33 KJV).

Father, we trust You for the basics of life but continue to worry about them,
as if our worrying could do us any good.
Strengthen our faith in Your provision so we can concentrate on
the work You have in mind for us to accomplish.

You know exactly what your children want for Christmas, don't you? And you will do your best to grant their wishes, no matter how long you have to stand in line or how expensive the toys. It's not that you are the best parents in the world, either!

As you limber up the credit cards over the next month to provide the "good gifts" your children request, remind yourself that your heavenly Father, the perfect parent, goes Christmas shopping every day of the year for you, answering your prayers, seeing to your needs, and doing it all out of His perfect love for you.

> If ye then,
> being evil,
> know how to give good gifts
> unto your children,
> how much more shall your Father
> which is in heaven give good things
> to them that ask him?
> MATTHEW 7:11 KJV

Father, we thank You for the love and attention You give us every day of our lives and for the precious gift of Your Son, our Savior.

_____THURSDAY_____

House and riches are
the inheritance of fathers:
and a prudent wife is
from the Lord.
PROVERBS 19:14 KJV

If you have ever come into some unexpected money, especially inherited money, you know how fast it can disappear without careful stewardship. A new home, a couple of cars, a visit from the IRS, and you're right back where you started. All those years of saving and going without wiped out in less than one generation!

On the other hand, money we make and save on our own, through prudent living and attention to details, we rarely waste. If you and your spouse are carefully saving for the future, you know why the writer of this psalm says a prudent wife is a gift from the Lord.

Father, we'll never be rich,
but we can be careful stewards of our financial resources,
with Your help.

Do you remember seeing old photos of early west-
ern plains settlers, all lined up in front of a sod
house with their children, horse, and dog? The
floor of the house was nothing but dirt, and the
walls and roof were sod. There were no windows; the
inside of the house was filled with smoke. It was shelter,
that's all. Until the ground was broken and the first crop planted, no one wasted time building a real house, because without a crop they would all die.

> Prepare thy work without,
> and make it fit for thyself in the field;
> and afterwards build thine house.
> PROVERBS 24:27 KJV

   We still need to prioritize today: first a job, then a lot of saving, then the house. Any
time you see your desires rushing ahead of your means, think of those pioneers and cut up
your credit cards.

*Father, set our priorities in order for us,
and give us the patience we need to realize our dreams one step at a time.*

_____SATURDAY_____

> A little sleep, a little slumber,
> a little folding of hands to rest,
> and poverty will come upon
> you like a vagabond,
> and want like an armed man.
> PROVERBS 6:10–11 RSV

December is not the time to rest, hands folded comfortably. With Christmas coming there is so much to do: cards to write, presents to buy and wrap, and family and church gatherings to attend.

But while doing all these things we also need to keep up with our jobs or other work. Attending too many parties and not taking care of business leads to unexpected job problems. Too much credit card use without the money to back it up will have us greeting January with a "woe is me" attitude as we open bills.

No one plans on poverty and want. People don't set them as life goals. But the daily elements of work and good budget management that keep us going financially keep them at bay.

Is God managing your life—or are you?

Lord, we want to manage responsibly all that You've given us.
Show us how to keep our money and lives in check.

Have you sent out Christmas cards yet? Probably not, unless you are extremely organized. This is a good time to keep in touch with friends and family you don't see regularly. Start planning now to present a warm Christmas greeting to the people you know and love, especially those you don't see often.

Perhaps you want to make this a time to share your faith in Christ. Together you may want to write a touching letter that shares what God has done for you this year or choose a holiday tract to include with your card.

If you need to gather together names and addresses for a Christmas card list, start today and do it together. Each of you knows different people who need to be on that list. One may remember a couple or family the other forgets. Once you've made up that list, save it for next year. With a few changes, you'll be ready to write next year's cards in no time!

_____MONDAY_____

> My soul finds rest in
> God alone;
> my salvation comes from him.
> PSALM 62:1 NIV

If our to-do list is longer than the days we have to accomplish things, we're *too* busy. Holidays can pull us into too many parties, special church occasions, and so on. Although all those things may be good, when they mount up and we become spiritually bedraggled by them, we've lost our balance in life.

True rest isn't attained in family parties, church meetings, or even good works. None of those offer the peace we're looking for. We can find true peace when we spend time with God. That may be in a special service, but we also need time together with Him in prayer and His Word. If we're attempting to do God's will without tapping directly into Him, we're out of His will, however busy we are.

We need to spend time today resting in Him alone.

Thank You, Lord, for being our rest.
When life gets too hectic,
remind us that we need to stop what we're doing and rest in You.

Within marriage we feel such mutual interconnectedness that over time we as partners become
difficult to separate. Think of one member of a
couple that's been married for years, and it may be
hard not to remember the other, too. When two people
who live together in marriage have the same goals, attitudes, and aims, we naturally connect them.

> I am my beloved's,
> and my beloved is mine. . . .
> SONG OF SOLOMON 6:3 NKJV

But this verse isn't only talking about the interconnectedness of two human lovers. The
Song of Solomon describes God's bride, the Church, as she shares love with Him.

As Christians, you are part of His Church—God's beloved. You are His, and He is
yours. Just as you closely identify with your spouse, God identifies with you. He connects
closely with those whom He loves.

Two who share both human love and God's love have the best of this world and the
next. Draw close to Him today.

Lord, thank You for such intimate love.
Draw us closer to You.

> Ram begot Amminadab,
> Amminadab begot Nahshon,
> and Nahshon begot Salmon.
> MATTHEW 1:4 NKJV

Run a computer spell check on *Amminadab* or *Nahshon* and you probably won't get any spelling options. Your machine can't recognize these as names of people who lived and made up part of Christ's earthly lineage, unless you add their names to your software's dictionary.

Unlike a computer, God recognizes people through the ages: the forgotten folk who did extraordinary works for Him, and those who struggled to do His will. People, perhaps, just like you.

A computer may not recognize your name, either, but God knows you, your day-to-day issues, and the works you do for Him. He joined you and your spouse together in marriage and knows each of you intimately. Every detail of your lives is open to Him, and He meets needs no computer could begin to touch.

You are loved deeply and satisfyingly by God. He's never forgotten you, and He never will.

Lord, thank You for remembering us, even when the world forgets.

"Don't make me come down there." Have you seen this little quote, signed "God"?

"The virgin will be with child and will give birth to a son, and they will call him Immanuel"— which means, "God with us."
MATTHEW 1:23 NIV

At this season, do we realize that Jesus' first coming wasn't a punishment? God didn't threaten to come down and set us straight, like small children who have irritated a parent.

Some people do fear God, like children who have been bad and expect punishment. They show it by avoiding Him year round. Even at Christmas they're unlikely to seek Him.

These folks have never intimately known the God who took on painful human form to give His life for them. He's not offering a threat but an eternal promise.

Father God, thank You for coming down,
not for punishment, but out of deep love.

> Put on the new self,
> which is being renewed in
> knowledge in the image of
> its Creator.
> COLOSSIANS 3:10 NIV

Many people would like to "redesign" Christmas into their own imaginary story. Maybe, they decide, Mary *wasn't* a virgin. Maybe Jesus was a she, not a He. Maybe He wasn't really God after all.

Maybe, maybe, maybe. Where do these flights of fancy get us? They certainly don't get us something new. Such often-recycled doubts won't profoundly change lives.

We can't recreate God in our own image and be happy. Wrong doctrine takes all the power out of faith and destroys God's ability to work in our lives.

Instead of falling for a bunch of *maybe*s, be renewed in the knowledge of God by believing just what He said about His plan for salvation and walking in that truth.

Then you'll be blessed with a new you, no *maybe*s about it.

Lord Jesus, thank You for coming to save us.
We want to believe in Your Christmas, not the imaginations of others.

_____

_____

_____

_____

_____

_____

_____

_____

_____

_____

_____

_____

Scripture doesn't tell us what words Mary used to explain this unusual event to Joseph. Although Luke describes her joyful acceptance of the news that she would bear God's Son, nowhere are we told of this most intimate conversation.

> After His mother Mary was betrothed to Joseph, before they came together, she was found with child of the Holy Spirit.
> MATTHEW 1:18 NKJV

Surely Mary must have been nervous. After all, Joseph knew he wasn't the father. How would he react? Though she knew her betrothed was a godly man and that God would help her, she must have felt a moment of nervousness. Could this ruin her relationship with her promised husband? Mary gave God wholehearted obedience anyway, trusting that bearing the Messiah would still be a blessing.

We've faced similar worrisome choices: *Will doing right be good for our marriage? Will God be there for us?*

If we follow Mary's example of implicit obedience, God comes through. Like her we can trust that He who calls us to obey also holds the future in His hands.

Lord, we want to obey You, no matter the cost.
Give us courage to do Your will.

So many traditions and stories have sprung up around Christmas. We should allow ourselves to enjoy them—unless they get in the way of the Good News God has to offer. The essence of Christmas is simply that God sent His Son to provide salvation for a sinful people.

What traditions do you associate with Christmas? Do they glorify God? If so, should you do something more to expand them? If not, how can you change them so they do honor Him? Should you be involved with them at all?

Are there some new traditions you need to start? Maybe you'd like to provide hospitality for some people who don't have anywhere to spend Christmas. Perhaps you'd like to give generously to a mission or ministry.

Together, discuss Christmas as you'd like it to be and how you can create more God-honoring celebrations.

What a kind, honest, God-fearing man was Joseph! Faced with the news that Mary was pregnant, he still loved her enough not to want to shame her. Knowing her baby wasn't his child, he wanted to do what was right before God. As her promised husband, he decided to follow the Law and divorce her, but quietly.

> Then Joseph, being aroused from sleep, did as the angel of the Lord commanded him and took to him his wife.
> MATTHEW 1:24 NKJV

How surprised he must have been when an angel visited him and told him to take Mary as his wife. Unhesitatingly, he obeyed, perhaps secretly joyous that Mary had not betrayed him.

Like Joseph, are you facing troubles? Do you still treat your spouse with kindness and gentleness? Or have you started an anger-kindling spat? Are trials your time to show your stuff or take it out on your spouse?

God blessed Joseph for his willingness to do what was right and the godly way he responded to trouble. Will He do any less for you?

Lord, when we face troubles, help us to respond in a way that honors You.

> Also the neighbor women gave him a name, saying, "There is a son born to Naomi." And they called his name Obed. He is the father of Jesse, the father of David.
>
> RUTH 4:17 NKJV

God's Word is full of unexpected blessings. Naomi, a woman whose life had become bitter because she'd lost her entire family, received the blessing of a grandson.

But Naomi's not the only blessed one. For Obed becomes part of the lineage of Jesus, the promised and long-expected Savior of all mankind. Out of Naomi's temporary sorrow came a blessing for the world. After all, if Naomi's daughter-in-law Ruth had never married her second husband, Obed could never have been born.

Are you and your spouse feeling very "unblessed" today? Perhaps that unexpected blessing from God is just around the corner. When it comes, His blessing may impact more than you and your family alone. People will call you blessed, if you remain faithful to Him in your trials.

Lord Jesus, we know Your blessings are at work in our lives.
Keep us faithful when we can't see them.

Christmas is a time for giving, but Scripture reminds us there's a way to give gifts and a way not to. You may not curry favor with a politician, but you can still give to impress or win favors. The problem is, the recipient's appreciation often lasts a short time and you can't reasonably give someone physical gifts every day.

Many curry favor with a ruler, and everyone is the friend of a man who gives gifts.
PROVERBS 19:6 NIV

When you buy your spouse a gift, are you trying to make up for some past error, impress him or her, or bend your husband's or wife's will on an issue you disagree on? If so, rethink your gift. Perhaps you really need to get one that will please without manipulating. Or maybe you need to work on a bad habit that irritates your spouse, be more faithful in carrying out promises, or do a chore every week without complaining. You can give that in addition to a physical gift and provide pleasure to your spouse all year long.

Lord, we want our gifts to please but not manipulate.
Let them reflect Your love.

_____ THURSDAY _____

> "But if you do not
> forgive men their sins,
> your Father will not
> forgive your sins."
> MATTHEW 6:15 NIV

One of those "Christmas spats," fueled by the tensions of holiday preparations, infiltrates your marriage. *How could he say that about my family?* you wonder. *If he doesn't want to be with them, he can't want to be with me!* It wasn't even a "big" sin, just a small thing that burned deeply into your heart.

Suddenly forgiveness, in this season that has so much to say on that subject, seems impossible. *Can God really mean I have to forgive that?* you start to wonder.

But He does. Jesus' example tells us unforgiveness is not an option. He paid a huge, painful price to enable us to forgive others, and to ignore that would be to ignore His greatest gift.

Don't let unforgiveness damage your life and relationships in this holy season. Instead let God's Spirit use your life in His work.

Lord Jesus, thank You for Your gift of forgiveness.
May it shine in our lives each day.

Even in a happy holiday season, troubles can come upon us. People may land in the hospital, lose a loved one, or have financial woes during a month when most hearts are light and God's blessings overflow. The merry season may make these things even harder to bear.

> God is our
> refuge and strength,
> a very present help in trouble.
> PSALM 46:1 NKJV

But the message of Christmas has less to do with carols, tinsel, and presents than the One who is ever present with us. Although friends or family may be cheerful while we're in the doldrums, we are not deserted. God has not forgotten us. Through it all, *He* is our refuge and strength, not the holiday season or traditions.

God hasn't stopped blessing you when troubles come. He becomes your blessing— there for you when you hurt and your protector from harm. When you turn aside from tinsel and celebrations, don't turn from the One who offers refuge at any season.

Thank You, Lord, for being our strength at any time
and for sending Your Son to show us the joy of Your love.

> "They have ascribed
> to David ten thousands,
> and to me they have
> ascribed but thousands.
> Now what more can he have
> but the kingdom?"
> So Saul eyed David
> from that day forward.
> 1 SAMUEL 18:8–9 NKJV

Jealous of the fame David had won in battle, King Saul began to look at Jesse's son as a threat to his throne. That jealousy ruined their relationship.

We don't have a throne to protect, but we do have relationships and a position in society that may be dear to us. During the holidays, if one of those is threatened, we may suddenly find ourselves doubtfully eyeing friends or family members.

Christmas can be tense for relationships. Perhaps we see more than usual of less-than-favorite family members. But let's not lose sight of why we celebrate. We aren't commemorating our position in society, the size of our gifts, or a special human relationship. Instead we're proclaiming God's love in sending His Son when we were unlovely, uncaring, and perhaps even rude.

We can share that with even the most difficult people.

Lord, help us share Your love with all whom we see this holiday—
even the ones who don't remind us most of You.

_____

_____

_____

_____

_____

_____

_____

_____

_____

_____

_____

How has God blessed you through this year? Have you faced some unusual trials or struggles? Or has life been unusually smooth? What do you have to praise Him for?

Spend some time together thinking about these questions.

1. How have you grown spiritually? Was it painful? Were the results worth it? What did you learn about God?

2. What physical trials have you gone through? Was God faithful? How did these trials strengthen your faith?

3. Have you been through financial trials? What did you learn about money? About God? How has this impacted your Christian walk?

4. With all these things, what have you been able to contribute to God's kingdom? Is there still more for you to accomplish, with God's help?

Finally, spend some time in prayer. Praise God for the good things He has done for you and the opportunities you have had for growth. Thank Him for being with you each step of the way.

*"'But you, Bethlehem,
in the land of Judah,
are by no means least among
the rulers of Judah;
for out of you will come a ruler
who will be the shepherd
of my people Israel.'"*
MATTHEW 2:6 NIV

Jesus doesn't look to enter only the world's important places. He wasn't born in Jerusalem, Israel's largest city, near important people. He came simply and quietly to the small place of God's promise, to Bethlehem.

He still doesn't pick the most exciting or important places or people. Jesus slips into hard hearts and into cold, dank places that have opened just a crack to Him, and creates of them a temple.

You may not describe your heart as a Jerusalem for God, but He's not asking for worldly greatness. Jerusalem, Israel's largest city, was not where Jesus was born but where He died an agonizing death.

He's looking for a stable that will receive Him, not a palace. Are you willing to become a temple in Bethlehem?

*Father God, thank You for sending Your Son into our hard hearts.
Make them places where You are worshiped.*

_____

_____

_____

_____

_____

_____

_____

_____

_____

_____

This is the same man speaking who asked an angel, "How shall I know this?" (v. 18). Zacharias's doubt turned to a glorious faith that shone in his prophecy about his son, John. Now that Zacharias saw God's "results," his faith burned strong. God could speak through him in a clear promise. But unbelief had silenced him for months.

> "And you, child, will be called the prophet of the Highest; for you will go before the face of the Lord to prepare His ways."
> LUKE 1:76 NKJV

If God were to prevent us from speaking when we lost faith, would we go months—or even years—in silence? By doubting His promises in Scripture or the still, small voice that leads us in His path, will we go down in Christian history as a pair of Zachariases?

God doesn't call us to believe when the child is born, but when it's conceived. He promises He'll bring something to pass, and we need to trust in Him for nine months.

But we don't need to wait that long to shout His praises.

Lord, we want to praise You today for Your plans for tomorrow.
Help us trust in You before we see every outcome.

Week 51

_____WEDNESDAY_____

> And, lo,
> the angel of the Lord
> came upon them,
> and the glory of the Lord
> shone round about them:
> and they were sore afraid.
> LUKE 2:9 KJV

Fear of God? That concept is foreign to many of us. We see God as our best buddy, as someone who would never hurt us. Painful things, some try to believe, *never* come from God.

True, God does not cause needless pain. He loves us deeply. Yet we often forget that pain often precedes growth, and a sinful human, confronted by pure holiness, is likely to feel the pain of inadequacy. One who has done wrong wants to run from Him who has never erred, even if He doesn't directly confront that sin.

Faced with the angel of the Lord, the shepherds quaked. They knew they could never measure up to God. If He held their sins against them, they had no recourse. After confronting them with His glory, God sent a small, helpless baby whom the shepherds could worship without fear. They could understand Him without running away.

Are you worshiping the Child—or are you on the run?

Lord God, we don't want to run from You.
We praise You for being our salvation.

Have you told others that God offers them peace, good things, and salvation? Or has your mouth been closed by fear?

Christmas is a time when people are confronted with Jesus. But many have never really heard the whole message He proclaims. Maybe they've sat in church services or seen a manger scene, but they've never known what God offers to them personally. It's not just an intellectual notion they can take or leave, but a life-changing message they need to respond to.

> How beautiful upon the mountains are the feet of him who brings good news, who proclaims peace, who brings glad tidings of good things, who proclaims salvation, who says to Zion, "Your God reigns!"
> ISAIAH 52:7 NKJV

Don't let Christmas pass without offering the Good News to someone. Pray about reaching out, and God will show you a need.

All you have to do is respond.

Lord, let us share this message with others as Christmas nears.
Give us Your words that will reach into hearts.

Week 51

FRIDAY____

> And it came to pass in those days that a decree went out from Caesar Augustus that all the world should be registered.
> LUKE 2:1 NKJV

When Caesar Augustus, one of Rome's greatest emperors, decreed that a census should be taken, all the empire moved to do his bidding.

As he made this decision, the Roman ruler was not thinking of obeying a God he didn't believe in. He had no knowledge of a promise made to a virgin or prophecies written in ancient texts. Yet his "independent" move brought to pass God's will.

When God is in charge, He brings amazing things to pass. People who don't even believe in Him may cause His will to happen for Christians. Seemingly impossible situations suddenly change. A knotty problem disappears.

When our lives are out of control, it's time to put them in the control of One who rules all, even the hearts of unbelieving emperors.

Lord, thank You for controlling our lives.
Work Your will in them today.

"Christmas is for children." "I most enjoy my children's excitement about gifts." You've probably heard such expressions. Maybe you've even used them.

Thanks be to God for his indescribable gift!
2 CORINTHIANS 9:15 NIV

Gifts have become part and parcel of Christmas. We say we're commemorating the gifts of the wise men, but is that really true? We also enjoy getting gifts. Without them, we have to admit, Christmas *would* be a disappointment.

Whether or not we can set the latest wrapped toys under the tree or buy our spouses the finest items, the real gift we need to celebrate is Jesus, who gave Himself to us. No present can match His impact on our otherwise empty lives.

Even if we can't spend a fortune on gifts, we can act like Jesus and become living presents who give our lives to those we love. We, too, can become indescribable gifts who touch the lives of needy, hurting souls.

That obedience may be the best gift of all.

Lord, help us to give, not only on December 25
but throughout the year, to glorify You and heal hurting hearts.

Is controlling your life important to you? Are you the kind who wants to be in charge of everything, or do you go with the flow? How does your mate answer these questions? Are the two of you different?

We can try to control our lives in many ways: spiritually, financially, organizationally, and so on. We certainly need to have some sense of where we are and where we're going. A completely out-of-control life is a poor Christian testimony, but so is a hypercontrolled one.

Are there some control issues that are hanging in your life? Together, try to identify them. Are they based on a lack of control or too much?

Ultimately, God should be in control of each area of your marriage and life together. If you've been in control and have not let Him rule in your lives, identify where you need to change and how you can do it. Set some plans in motion today.

Joseph and Mary were obeying God when, at a time when any woman would be wise not to travel far, they packed up and visited Bethlehem.

> He went there to register with Mary, who was pledged to be married to him and was expecting a child.
> LUKE 2:5 NIV

How easy it might have been for the couple to complain—wasn't this babe the most important one in the world? *Lord, it isn't safe for a woman close to the end of her pregnancy to travel so far,* Mary might have objected. Instead, they did what was put before them without complaint.

That simple obedience had a powerful result. Through that move, God fulfilled Micah 5:2, that Israel's ruler would be born in Bethlehem, not Nazareth.

When "life" seems to interrupt your plans, do you complain or adapt? Can you see it as part of God's plan, and not just an irritant? God might use that interruption to create a great moment in your life.

Lord, use every interruption in our lives to Your glory.

> For to us a child is born,
> to us a son is given,
> and the government will be
> on his shoulders.
> ISAIAH 9:6 NIV

A babe born in a manger to a couple of peasants who had no claim to greatness hardly seems the fulfillment of this prophecy of a gift to a whole nation—and ultimately the world.

But "for to us a child is born," not just to Mary, Joseph, and even God the Father. Jesus' birth was a gift to an entire sinful world, one that often places much emphasis on how much stature Mom and Dad have in the community or what their bank balance is.

That one, small child, humble and helpless, would rule the world as no king's son or daughter could. No child of wealthy parents could accomplish His deeds.

Jesus, the gift straight from God, reaches places in the soul no human goes. Small and pitiable on the outside on the night of His birth, inside He still held all the answers to every human need.

We need never be ruled by anyone else.

Lord, rule in our hearts this Christmas and every day of the year.

For wise men, these don't seem very astute. Walking into a king's palace and asking about another king seems to be looking for trouble.

The men from the East may have had some wisdom, but they couldn't read minds. They obviously didn't know the full situation, and they didn't know a thing about wicked King Herod.

Now after Jesus was born in Bethlehem. . . in the days of Herod the king. . . wise men from the East came to Jerusalem, saying, "Where is He who has been born King of the Jews?"
Matthew 2:1–2 NKJV

Even the wisest human beings cannot know everything. Extremely discerning folks still make mistakes because they don't have enough information.

The only wisdom that never fails is from God, and because the wise men's hearts were right and they were obeying Him, He guided them away from danger and kept His Son safe.

Like those men, we don't have to rely on our own abilities. We can seek wisdom far greater than ours in God. Have you done that together today?

Lord, give us Your wisdom. On our own, we will only fail.

An angel of the Lord
appeared to Joseph in a dream, saying,
"Arise, take the young Child and His mother,
flee to Egypt,
and stay there until I bring you word;
for Herod will seek the young Child
to destroy Him."
MATTHEW 2:13 NKJV

God not only watched over Jesus' birth with stars and angels, He looked after His Son when danger threatened from a wicked ruler.

Jesus' birth, followed by a sudden death, would not have saved God's people. There was work for Him to do, and God saw it through to completion. No threatening danger changed His plan.

Just as God looked after Jesus, He also looks after you. He's created you for a purpose in this world and will see that purpose through to completion. So when money is short, you face a dozen challenges, or relationships seem stressed, remember, God is not finished.

Two thousand years ago He watched over His Son, protected Him, and made His will plain. Today He also watches over His adopted children. Whether He directs you to flee or stand firm, He'll keep you safe.

Thank You, Lord, for daily protection as we do Your will.
Help us to stand firm.

Sending Jesus and His earthly parents into exile in Egypt was only a temporary measure of protection. Living there, Jesus could never have brought the message of salvation to God's people. He had to live with them, learn their ways, and be one of them.

> "When Israel was a child, I loved him, and out of Egypt I called My son."
> HOSEA 11:1 NKJV

God didn't call the holy family back to Nazareth because it was convenient to Mary or Joseph, or even Jesus. God loved Israel and wanted to save the people of His covenant. His purpose wouldn't be fulfilled if the three stayed in a foreign land.

In marriage, God sometimes calls us out of protected places into places of action. They may not be comfortable, and they often aren't the places we thought we'd be in. Staying in our nice, comfy spots seems more desirable. But like Mary and Joseph, obedience to God requires that we answer the uncomfortable call.

After the struggle, the blessings we reap will have a value far beyond the troubles we've faced.

Father God, sometimes Your call doesn't seem convenient to us.
We want to obey You anyway.

_____SATURDAY_____

> "Sovereign Lord,
> as you have promised,
> you now dismiss your servant in peace.
> For my eyes have seen
> your salvation."
> LUKE 2:29–30 NIV

God keeps His promises: the ones He makes to us personally and the ones He's made to the world and spoken through Scripture.

In this passage, the Father had just shown His faithfulness by fulfilling a centuries-old promise that He made to the Jews as soon as Adam fell. A Savior would redeem them. But He also fulfilled a personal promise to a man named Simeon whom the Holy Spirit had promised would see the infant Savior.

As you face a new year, are you confident God will keep His promises? When God makes them, it's not just in the abstract. He means His promises for people—all of us who believe in Him.

If you can trust that He gave us His Son, you can trust Him when He moves you to change jobs, take on a spiritual risk, or give unselfishly. He hasn't broken a promise yet, and He won't start with you.

Thank You, God, for Your faithfulness to every promise.
We can trust in You.

_____
_____
_____
_____
_____
_____
_____
_____
_____
_____
_____
_____
_____
_____
_____
_____
_____
_____
_____
_____

Is obedience hard for you? Does it seem inconvenient and irritating, or do you enjoy obeying God?

Chances are, if you are honest, it's sometimes one and sometimes the other. Some of the plans God has for you seem pleasant, while others bring you fear.

Read Luke 1–2:7. Compare Zechariah's response with the responses of Mary and Joseph. What can you learn from each? Pay special attention to Mary's words of praise to God in Luke 1:46–55. What does her response tell you about her attitude?

What challenges to obedience do each of you face? Discuss those things that make it hard for you and how you can overcome them. Then spend time together in prayer, seeking the solutions God has to offer.